INHALT CONTENTS SOMMAIRE

6 Vorwort	6 Preface	6 Préface
9 Kleine Lichtgeschichte	9 A short history of light	9 Petite histoire de la lumière
26 Technikbrevier	26 Short technical guide	26 Petit manuel technique
31 **Pendelleuchten**	31 **Pendant lights**	31 **Lampes suspendues**
65 **Wand- und Deckenleuchten**	65 **Wall and ceiling lights**	65 **Appliques et plafonniers**
77 **Stehleuchten**	77 **Standard lamps**	77 **Lampadaires**
103 **Tischleuchten**	103 **Table lamps**	103 **Lampes de table**
131 **Niedervolt- und Systemleuchten**	131 **Low-voltage and system lighting**	131 **Lampes basse tension et systèmes d'éclairage sur rails**
141 **Bodenleuchten und Lichtobjekte**	141 **Floor lighting and design objects**	141 **Lampes de sol et objets lumineux**
158 **Hersteller und Bezugsquellen**	158 **Manufacturers and retailers**	158 **Fabricants et fournisseurs**
160 **Index**	160 **Index**	160 **Index**

VORWORT

Wallwasher, Downlight-Systeme, Kaltlicht-reflektoren, Blendschutzklappen, UV-Ab-sorber, Niedervoltlampen, Natriumdampf-Hochdrucktechnik, Floodlinsen und Kreuzraster – wer heute eine passende Lampe für seine Wohnung sucht, trifft im Fachhandel auf eine derart erschlagende Fülle an technischen Innovationen, daß er sich ohne ingenieurwissenschaftliche Fach-kenntnisse verloren glaubt. Daß man auf dem Lampenmarkt heute viel Expertenwis-sen braucht, rührt auch daher, daß viele Neuerungen, die ursprünglich für den indu-striellen und gewerblichen Bereich, für Re-klame, Verkaufs-, Messe- und Bürobe-leuchtung bestimmt waren, auch immer häufiger in Wohnungen verwendet wer-den. Vor allem die Halogentechnik, die zu-erst im Automobilbau und in der Bühnen- und Filmszenographie eingesetzt wurde, hat viele Wohnzimmer in halbprofessionel-le Kunstlichtstudios verwandelt.

So erfährt die künstliche Beleuchtung in den Wohnungen eine ähnliche technische Aufrüstung wie die Audio-Video-Geräte der Hifi-Industrie. Doch die immer phantasti-scheren Daten und Leistungen, die immer perfekteren Wiedergabe- und Manipu-lationsqualitäten gehen über den realen Be-darf der Konsumenten meist weit hinaus. Die technische Überinstrumentierung ver-stellt den Blick auf elementare Gebrauchs-qualitäten.

Auch in der Designgeschichte findet die Leuchtengestaltung nur als Randerschei-nung Erwähnung. Das liegt an der einseiti-gen Überbetonung des Mobiliars und der Materialeigenschaften der Gebrauchsge-genstände. Das immaterielle Phänomen der Lichterzeugung entzieht sich der stilisti-schen Klassifikation. Und seit der Revolu-tion der Halogen- und Systemlampen der sechziger Jahre, die die Lichterzeugung immer mehr entmaterialisierten und die Lichtquellen dezentralisierten,richtet sich die Lichtfrage auf ingenieurtechnische Details.

Das vorliegende Buch will das Augenmerk wieder auf die Form und Gestalt der

PREFACE

Wallwashers, downlight systems, cold-beam reflectors, anti-glare shutters, UV-absorbers, low-voltage lamps, sodium gas discharge lights, floodlights and profiled lamellae - nowadays, anyone looking for a suitable lamp for home use is confronted with such an overwhelming abundance of technical innovations in specialist shops that he feels at a loss without some know-ledge of engineering. The need for expert knowledge of the light-market is partly due to the fact that many innovations which were originally intended for industrial and commercial use, for advertising, trade-fair and office purposes are finding increasing application in the home. Above all the hal-ogen light, initally used in the car industry and for stage and film lighting, has now changed many a living-room into a semi-professional light studio.

Artificial lighting in the home is experien-cing a technical boost similar to that of audio and video apparatus in the hi-fi indus-try. Yet the increasingly fantastic data and performance, the increasing perfection of reproduction and manipulability far surpass the consumer's actual requirements. Such excessive technical instrumentation has obscured the original purpose for buying a light.

Lamp design appears only as a fringe phe-nomenon within the history of design. This is due to the exaggerated stressing of fur-niture and the material qualities of house-hold goods. The immaterial phenomenon of producing light eludes stylistic classifica-tion. Indeed, since the revolution of hal-ogen and system lighting in the 'Sixties, which dematerialised the production of light and decentralized the source, the question of light has become one of technical details.

This book attempts to direct our attention back to the shape and design of lights as a fundamental element of furnishing. Light sources are usually only perceived as back-ground phenomena, and yet they are one of the most important pieces of furniture because they are most often used,

PRÉFACE

Il faut être aujourd'hui au moins ingénieur de formation pour affronter sans craintes les nouveautés techniques que nous pré-sentent les magasins spécialisés dans l'éclairage. Gare à celui qui cherche une lampe pour son appartement: on ne lui parle que de wallwashers, downlight-sys-tems, réflecteurs à lumière froide, volets antiéblouissants, absorbeurs de rayons ultraviolets, lampes basse tension, lampes à vapeur de sodium à haute pression, pro-jecteurs d'ambiance et paralumes cruci-formes. Le fait que de nombreuses nouveautés, prévues au départ pour l'in-dustrie et le commerce, les espaces publi-citaires, l'éclairage de points de vente, de salons commerciaux et de bureaux fassent de plus en plus souvent leur entrée dans les appartements explique le niveau de connaissances requises en ce domaine. Ceci est particulièrement vrai pour l'éclai-rage halogène, d'abord utilisé dans la con-struction automobile, sur les scènes de théâtre et dans les décors de cinéma, et qui a transformé de nombreuses salles de séjour en véritables studios de profession-nels.

L'éclairage artificiel des appartements fait l'objet d'un perfectionnement technique constant semblable à celui que l'on ob-serve dans le domaine de l'industrie hi-fi. Mais si les caractères techniques et les performances des chaînes et systèmes vidéo sont de plus en plus fantastiques, leurs qualités de manipulation et de re-transmission toujours plus parfaites, ils dépassent le plus souvent les besoins réels des consommateurs. La survalorisa-tion technique des appareils empêche de voir leurs qualités élémentaires d'utilisa-tion.

L'histoire du design accorde une impor-tance prépondérante au mobilier et aux qualités matérielles des objets, elle ne mentionne donc qu'en passant les formes des lampes. La naissance de la lumière, phénomène non matériel, se dérobe à une classification stylistique. Et depuis l'appari-tion des lampes halogènes et des sys-

300
Lights · Leuchten · Lampes

MATTHIAS DIETZ · MICHAEL MÖNNINGER

BENEDIKT TASCHEN VERLAG

UMSCHLAGVORDERSEITE / FRONT COVER / COUVERTURE

WG 24
Design Wilhelm Wagenfeld 1924

PH-Kugel-Lamell
Design Poul Henningsen 1958

One from the Heart
Design Ingo Maurer 1989

Ara
Design Philippe Starck 1988

SCHMUTZTITEL / FLY TITLE / PAGE DU GARDE

Luigi
Design Borek Sipek
Driade
6 x 50 Watt
H 80 cm, B 50 cm, ø 60 cm

FRONTISPIZ / FRONTISPIECE / FRONTISPICE

Costanza
Design Paolo Rizzatto 1986
Luceplan
150 Watt
H 120 - 160 cm, ø 40 cm

UMSCHLAGRÜCKSEITE / BACK COVER / AU DOS

PH 4-3 Table Lamp
Design Poul Henningsen 1966

Tizio
Design Richard Sapper 1990

Metro
Design Hannes Wettstein 1982

Contacto
Design Jürgen Medebach 1990

Corona
Design Vincenzo Porcelli 1987

Borea
Design David Palterer 1991

Glühwürmchen
Design Stiletto Studios 1990

Pflanzlicht
Design Stiletto Studios 1990

Copylight Edition Kopie
Design Meta Moderne,
Dietz Design Management 1993

© 1993 Benedikt Taschen Verlag GmbH
Hohenzollernring 53, D-50672 Köln

© 1993 VG Bild-Kunst, Bonn, for the works by Man Ray,
Gerrit Rietveld and Frank Schreiner

Edited by Matthias Dietz, Frankfurt
Text: Michael Mönninger, Frankfurt
Design: Rafael Jiménez & Claudia Casagrande, Frankfurt
Text edited by Simone Philippi, Cologne
English translation: Melanie Girdlestone, Munich
French translation: Michèle Schreyer, Cologne
Production: Boris Niedieck, Cologne
Reproductions: ORD, Gronau

Printed in Germany
ISBN 3-8228-9450-8

Leuchte als elementarem Bestandteil des Mobiliars richten. Lichtquellen werden meist nur als Hintergrundphänomene wahrgenommen. Dabei zählen sie zu den wichtigsten Einrichtungsgegenständen, weil sie am häufigsten benutzt, ein- und ausgeschaltet, immer wieder neu positioniert werden und die Anmutung der Innenarchitektur maßgeblich bestimmen. Dieses Buch will einen Marktüberblick schaffen und durch Auswahl und Wertung eine Entscheidungshilfe bieten. Die dreihundert präsentierten Lampen und Objekte stellen zwar eine subjektive Auswahl dar, aber in repräsentativer Absicht. Wir streben keine Vollständigkeit an, sondern eine exemplarische Darstellung der besten und wichtigsten Leuchten auf dem gegenwärtigen Markt. Voraussetzung für die Aufnahme der Modelle in dieses Buch war, daß sie heute produziert werden und im Einzelhandel verfügbar sind. Weil diese aktuelle Designgeschichte der Beleuchtung in praktischer Absicht verfaßt wurde, weist sie, vor allem was großmaßstäbliche Expertenlichtsysteme angeht, zwangsläufig Lücken und Vorlieben auf. Das war nicht nur unvermeidlich, sondern auch beabsichtigt.

switched on or off or moved around, and they are decisive in determining the quality of an interior. This book aims to supply an overview of the market and provide help in decision making through its selection and evaluation of possibilities. The three hundred lamps and designs presented here are indeed a subjective selection, but they are intended to be representative. Our aim is not comprehensiveness but an illustrative presentation of the best and most important lights on the market today. One requirement for the inclusion of the models in this book was that they are in production at the moment and available at the retailer's. Since this current history of lamp design was written with practical intentions, there are inevitably omissions as well as preferences, above all where large-scale expert lighting systems are concerned. This was not only unavoidable but also intentional.

tèmes d'éclairage révolutionnaires des années 60, qui dématérialisent la lumière et multiplient ses sources, la lumière devient de plus en plus technique.
Le présent livre veut réattirer notre attention sur l'aspect et la forme des lampes perçues en tant qu'éléments de base du mobilier. Les sources lumineuses sont considérées le plus souvent comme un phénomène de second plan. Pourtant les lampes sont des meubles à part entière, c'est elles qu'on utilise le plus: on les allume, on les éteint, on les déplace sans cesse et elles déterminent en grande mesure les impressions que nous avons d'un intérieur. Ce livre veut donner au lecteur une idée d'ensemble et l'aider à faire son choix. Les 300 objets et lampes présentés ici à titre d'exemple expriment, il est vrai, un choix subjectif mais qui se veut représentatif. On peut trouver tous les modèles chez les détaillants. Cette histoire du design de l'éclairage est avant tout un guide pratique, elle présente donc nécessairement, surtout en ce qui concerne les systèmes d'éclairage spécialisés à grande échelle, des lacunes et des préférences. Effet non seulement inévitable mais aussi recherché.

FILO DI FERRO

Design Dal Mondo 1992
Mondo
H 122 cm, ø 114 cm
gebogener Draht
Bended wire
Fil de fer recoubré

KLEINE LICHTGESCHICHTE

A SHORT HISTORY OF LIGHT

PETITE HISTOIRE DE LA LUMIERE

Die ergiebigste Lichtquelle der Welt befindet sich 149,6 Millionen Kilometer von der Erde entfernt, hat einen Durchmesser von 1,4 Millionen Kilometern und strahlt fortwährend eine Energiemenge von 6450 Watt pro Quadratzentimeter ab. Alles, was seit Entstehung der Sonne an weiteren Lichtquellen erfunden wurde, wäre nicht der Rede wert, gäbe es nicht den Hang der Menschen, alles Natürliche in sein Gegenteil zu verkehren. Um die Nacht zum Tag, das Innen zum Außen, den Schatten zur Helle, die Lüge zur Wahrheit und das Profane zum Sakralen zu machen, haben die Menschen immer neue Möglichkeiten der künstlichen Beleuchtung erfunden.

Das Urmotiv des Kunstlichts liegt in Kultus und Religion. Der Kunsthistoriker Hans Sedlmayr hat in seiner Studie »Das Licht in seinen künstlerischen Manifestationen« die artifizielle Illumination aus den Zauberkulten, Mysterien und Feiern in altsteinzeitlichen Höhlen hergeleitet, wo Tiermalereien beim flackernden Feuer scheinbar zum Leben erweckt wurden.[1] Später erhellten Fackeln, Kerzen und Öllampen antike Tempel, um das göttliche, übernatürliche Licht des Jenseits einzufangen. Und in den letzten Höhlen, den fensterlosen Theatern des Barock, trat das Licht endgültig in den Dienst einer weltlichen Magie: der Bühne und der Kunst. Daraus hat sich seit der Elektrifizierung der Geist der Ausstellung, des Schaufensters und der Reklame entwickelt.

Jeder vorsätzliche Gebrauch der elektromagnetischen Energiewellen namens Licht läßt sich heute im Grunde auf zwei Zwecke zurückführen: entweder auf die Kunst oder den Kommerz. Das ist das genaue Gegenteil der Lichtmetaphysik und Lichtmetaphorik der abendländischen Philosophie, die stets vom Urbild der unverfälschten Sonne ausgeht, in deren Licht allein die reine, nackte Wahrheit aufscheint. »Die Erkenntnis umreißt wie die Sonne erst auf der Höhe ihrer Bahn die Dinge am strengsten«,[2] faßte Walter Benjamin diese erkenntnistheoretische Sonnenphilosophie zusammen.

The most powerful source of light in the world is 149.6 million kilometres away from the earth, is 1.4 million kilometres in diameter and, through its peaceful use of nuclear power, radiates a constant 6450 watts of energy per square centimetre. All other light sources invented since the genesis of the sun would not be worth mentioning were it not for man's innate tendency to turn everything natural into its opposite. Be it to turn night into day, inside into out, shadow into light, lies into truth or the profane into the sacred, man has always invented new possibilities of artificial light. Following the natural examples of the sun, lightning, and glow-worms man has developed incandescence, electrical discharge and luminous power, which he has mostly used for rather shady purposes.

The original motive for producing artificial light lies in religion and cult worship. In a study entitled »Das Licht in seinen künstlerischen Manifestationen« (»Light in Its Artistic Manifestations«) the art historian Hans Sedlmayr has traced the derivation of artificial light back to magical cults, mysteries and ceremonies held in caves in the Old Stone Age, where animal paintings would appear to come to life in the flickering firelight.[1] Later torches, candles and oil-lamps illuminated ancient temples in order to capture the divine, supernatural light of the other world. In the most modern caves, the windowless theatres of the Baroque era, light finally came to serve the purposes of a secular magic: of the stage and of art. Since electrification, this has developed into the spirit of exhibitions, window-displays and advertising.

Each deliberate use of those electromagnetic energy waves we call light can essentially be traced back to two purposes today: art or commerce. This is a radical contradiction of the metaphysics of light and its metaphoric significance in Western philosophy, where the sun represents absolute purity in whose light the untarnished and naked truth shines. Walter Benjamin summarised the epistemological philo-

La plus abondante source de lumière dont nous disposons se trouve à 149,6 millions de kilomètres de la Terre, elle a un diamètre de 1,4 millions de kilomètres et rayonne une puissance de 6450 watts au centimètre carré. Toutes les autres sources de lumière découvertes depuis la naissance du Soleil ne vaudraient pas la peine d'être mentionnées, si les hommes ne cherchaient pas toujours à reproduire et inverser les phénomènes naturels. Pour transformer la nuit en jour, l'intérieur en extérieur, l'ombre en lumière, le mensonge en vérité et le profane en sacré, ils ont sans cesse trouvé de nouveaux moyens de créer la lumière articielle.

A l'origine de la lumière articielle, on trouve d'abord le culte et la religion. Dans son étude sur «La Lumière et ses manifestations artistiques» l'historien d'art Hans Sedlmayr fait remonter l'origine de l'éclairage artificiel des cultes magiques, des Mystères et des fêtes au fait que dans les grottes préhistoriques les animaux peints sur les parois semblaient vivre à la lueur des flammes.[1] Plus tard, des flambeaux, des bougies et des lampes à huile éclairèrent les temples antiques pour capter la lumière divine et surnaturelle de l'Au-delà. Et dans les théâtres dépourvus de fenêtres de l'ère baroque qui sont nos dernières grottes, la Lumière se mit définitivement au service d'une magie profane, celle de la scène et de l'art. C'est sur cette base que s'est développée l'idée de l'exposition, de la vitrine et de la publicité depuis que notre monde connaît l'électricité.

Force est de constater que toute utilisation préméditée de ces ondes électromagnétiques que nous appelons Lumière ne sert que deux objectifs: l'art ou le commerce. Exactement le contraire de ce que nous apprend la philosophie orientale qui part toujours de l'image première d'un Soleil authentique, dans la seule lumière duquel apparaît la Vérité pure et nue. «Ce n'est qu'au point le plus élevé de son cours que la Connaissance, comme le Soleil, trace les contours les plus précis des choses.»[2]

Auch Nietzsche sah seinen Zarathustra als Denker im »Lebensmittag« und im »Sommergarten«, der die Wahrheit ohne Kunstlicht und Schlagschatten sucht.
Genauso wichtig wie die Geschichte des künstlichen Lichts ist auch die des Umgangs mit dem Naturlicht. Sie muß aber erst noch geschrieben werden. Das Biegen und Brechen der Sonnenstrahlen beginnt beim antiken Atriumhaus mit seinen Lichthöfen und setzt sich architekturgeschichtlich im Bau von Oberlichtern und Fenstern fort. Die großartigsten Beispiele dafür sind das schlichte große Lichtauge des antiken Pantheons in Rom und die fast völlig in Glasfenster aufgelösten Wände der gotischen Sainte Chapelle in Paris.
Erst spät in der Moderne taucht der Wunsch nach unverfälschtem Naturlicht im Zeichen eines neuen Primitivismus wieder auf. Le Corbusier schätzte den Purismus der romanischen Wand und die Schatten der tiefen Laibung.[3] Mit Loggien, Sonnenblenden und Schotten schuf er Lichtschächte, um Innenräume durch gebündelte Strahlen und Außenflächen durch Schattenprofile zu konturieren. Dem Verwandlungszauber des Kunstlichts mißtraute er, weil es seine scharfkantigen Tageslichtskulpturen in unkontrollierbare Scheingebilde aufgelöst hätte.
Ähnlich kunstlichtfeindlich war auch der Amerikaner Frank Lloyd Wright. Anstelle der perforierten Bauvolumina der europäischen Bautradition mit ihren erzwungenen künstlichen Beleuchtungen bevorzugte er den unbehinderten Lichtfluß durch die Zwischenräume freistehender Wand- und Deckenscheiben, die im Gegensatz zum beengenden Lochfenster unbegrenzte Raumkontinuität schaffen sollten. Und nach der klassischen Moderne war es der Amerikaner Louis Kahn, der seine Architektur als Lichtmodulator ohne pittoreske Elemente und ohne Kunstlicht entwarf. Sein Credo war: »Licht ist belebte Materie.« Künstliche Beleuchtungen widersprachen für ihn dem Rhythmus des natürlichen Lichtwechsels.[4]

sophy of the sun as follows: »Cognition, like the sun, delineates things most clearly when it is at its highest point.«[2]
Nietzsche, too, saw his Zarathustra as a thinker at his »life's noon« in the »summer garden«, searching for the truth without artificial light and shadows. It is no mere coincidence that the highest level of human cognition is called »enlightenment« in the Far East, where truth is cherished.
The history of our treatment of natural light is equally as important as the history of our attitude to artificial light. Such a history, however, has yet to be written. Refraction and splitting of light began in the ancient atria and continued with the construction of windows. The greatest examples of this are the simple great »eye« of light in the dome of the ancient Pantheon in Rome and the predominantly glass walls of the Gothic Sainte Chapelle in Paris.
It was only later in the modern period that there was a renewed desire for natural and unadulterated light, a desire which arose against the background of a new primitivism. Le Corbusier admired the purism of the wall in Romanesque architecture with the shadows of its deep recesses.[3] Using loggias, shades and slit windows he created shafts of light. He thus shaped interiors by concentrating streams of light, and outlined exterior surfaces using profiles and shadows. He mistrusted the variform magic of artificial light, which would have made his sharp day-light sculptures dissolve into uncontrollable illusions.
Another opponent of artificial light was the American Frank Lloyd Wright. Instead of the perforated block architecture of the European tradition, in which artificial light was a necessity, he preferred the free flow of light between free-standing walls and ceilings which, unlike the restrictive »perforated« windows, would lend his buildings an unlimited continuity of space. At the most he would accept the open fire as an interior light source and central meeting-place. A successor of classical modern designers was the American Louis Kahn, who

C'est ainsi que Walter Benjamin résume cette philosophie solaire précédant une théorie de la Connaissance. Le Zarathoustra de Nietzsche est, lui aussi, un penseur au «zénith de la vie» et dans le «jardin estival», il cherche la Vérité sans lumière artificielle et sans zones d'ombre.
L'histoire des rapports entre l'Homme et la lumière naturelle est tout aussi importante que l'histoire de la lumière artificielle. Mais nul n'a encore songé à l'écrire. Déjà, dans l'atrium antique, on cherche à courber et rompre les rayons solaires, plus tard on construira des impostes et des fenêtres. Le grand œil de lumière du Panthéon romain et les vitraux où disparaissent presque les murs de la Sainte-Chapelle gothique à Paris illustrent ces efforts de manière grandiose.
Il faut attendre l'époque moderne pour que renaisse le souhait d'une lumière naturelle non falsifiée sous le signe d'un nouveau primitivisme. Le Corbusier apprécie le purisme du mur romain et les ombres des profonds intrados.[3] A l'aide de loggias, de parasols et de cloisons il crée des puits au jour mettant en valeur les cours intérieures en leur donnant des contours ombragés au moyen de faisceaux lumineux et de surfaces extérieures. Il se méfie de la lumière articielle qui dilue les arêtes vives de ses sculptures de lumière diurne, les métamorphosant en apparitions irréelles impossibles à maîtriser.
L'Américain Frank Lloyd Wright est, lui aussi, un ennemi de la lumière artificielle. Il dédaigne les volumes perforés de la tradition architecturale européenne aux éclairages artificiels forcés, leur préférant les panneaux isolés servant de murs et de plafonds où passe le flot lumineux ininterrompu, ce qui crée une continuité spatiale non délimitée contrairement à la fenêtre-perforation rétrécissante. Et après les modernes classiques, l'Américain Louis Kahn crée une architecture modelant la lumière sans éléments pittoresques et sans éclairage artificiel, fidèle à sa devise: «La Lumière est la matière animée.» Pour lui

Die neuesten Techniken zur Verwendung von Naturlicht sind heute die diaphanen Glasfassaden und Fensterfilter in Bauten von Norman Foster, Richard Rogers oder Peter Eisenman. Sie fangen entweder als weiterentwickelter »Curtain-Wall« direkt die Sonne auf und filtern sie. Oder sie sammeln das Licht auf dem indirekten Wege der Tageslichtumlenkung mit Sonnenschaufeln und Reflektoren vor der Fassade ein und leiten es nach innen weiter.

VON DER TECHNIK ZUM STIL

Der Kampf moderner Puristen gegen den eitlen Lichtzauber ist verständlich, wenn man sich die Allgewalt und Unerbittlichkeit vergegenwärtigt, mit der sich das Licht, die Technik und die große Industrie im Alltagsleben breitgemacht haben. Die Industrialisierung der Beleuchtung begann um 1800 in England mit der Gasgewinnung aus Kokereien. Zuvor waren alle Leuchtkörper selbständige Einheiten gewesen. Durch die Vernetzung der Energiegewinnung wurde jede einzelne Brennstelle von der zentralen städtischen Gasanstalt abhängig. Doch erst die Elektrifizierung schuf den totalen Systemzwang der Energieversorgung, weil das Leitungsnetz erstmals große Entfernungen überbrücken konnte.[5]
Als Erfinder der ersten Glühlampe gilt Heinrich Goebel, ein nach New York ausgewanderter Uhrmacher aus Hannover. 1854 hatte er eine verkohlte Bambusfaser in einem weitgehend luftleeren Parfümfläschchen zum Glühen gebracht, was er aber mangels Stromnetzes nur zur Beleuchtung seines Schaufensters in New York verwenden konnte. Thomas Alva Edison gebührt das Verdienst, die Erfindung zur Serienreife und zu einem großtechnischen System mit Leitungsnetz und Dauerversorgung entwickelt zu haben.[6] Von 1879 an stellte er in New York die ersten brauchbaren Glühlampen industriell her und prophezeite: »Wir werden das elektrische Licht so billig machen, daß sich nur noch reiche Leute eine Kerze werden leisten können.«[7]

intended his buildings to be modulators of light free of picturesque elements or artificial illumination. His credo was: »Light is living material.« He considered artificial lighting a contradiction of the natural, rhythmic change of light.[4]
Nowadays, the most modern methods of using natural light are the diaphanous glass facades and filter windows in the buildings of Norman Foster, Richard Rogers or Peter Eisenmann. They either act as a further development of the »curtain wall«, catching the sunlight directly and filtering it, or they collect light indirectly using sun-traps and reflectors positioned in front of the facade and redirect it to the interior. Examples of this are Norman Foster's Hong Kong Bank or the reflector labyrinths of the lighting designer Christian Bartenbach from Innsbruck.

FROM TECHNOLOGY TO STYLE

The struggle of modern purists against the vain illusionism of light becomes understandable when one thinks of the omnipotence and relentlessness with which light, technology and mass industry have pervaded daily life. The industrialization of lighting began in England around 1800 with the production of gas in coking plants. Until then all lamps had functioned as independent units. The construction of a gas network made every single lamp dependent on the central municipal gasworks. Only with electrification, however, did absolute reliance on the supply system become necessary, since the cable network was now able to span long distances.[5]
The inventor of the first electric light-bulb is said to be Heinrich Goebel, a clock-maker from Hannover who had emigrated to New York. In 1854 he had managed to make a charred bamboo fibre glow in a vacuum-sealed perfume bottle. However, as there was no electricity network, he could only use it to light his shop window in New York. It was Thomas Alva Edison who deserves the credit for having developed the invention into a highly technical system

l'éclairage artificiel contredit le rythme de la lumière.[4]
Les façades de verre diaphanes et les fenêtres-filtres des bâtiments construits par Norman Foster, Richard Rogers et Peter Eisenman représentent les techniques les plus récentes pour exploiter la lumière naturelle. Soit elles captent directement les rayons du soleil et les filtrent comme un mur rideau très évolué, ou elles recueillent indirectement la lumière diurne en la déviant à l'aide de collecteurs solaires et de réflecteurs placés devant la façade, et la dirigent ensuite à l'intérieur.

DE LA TECHNIQUE AU STYLE

Face à la violence et l'intransigeance qu'ont manifestées la lumière, la technique et l'industrie en s'établissant dans la vie quotidienne, on comprend aisément que les puristes modernes luttent contre la vanité de la magie lumineuse. L'éclairage industriel a fait son apparition en Angleterre vers 1800, lorsqu'on a commencé à obtenir du gaz de cokerie. Auparavant tous les corps lumineux étaient des unités autonomes. Une fois le réseau de distribution achevé, chaque point d'éclairage dépend de l'usine à gaz municipale. Mais l'électrification va vraiment asservir la société, car, pour la première fois, le réseau de distribution peut surmonter de grandes distances.[5]
Heinrich Goebel, un horloger de Hanovre émigré à New York, est considéré comme l'inventeur de la première lampe à incandescence. En 1854 il réussit à faire rougir une fibre de bambou carbonisée placée dans un flacon de parfum vide d'air, mais faute de courant électrique il ne peut l'utiliser que pour éclairer sa vitrine à New York. Thomas Edison perfectionne cette découverte jusqu'à ce qu'on puisse l'industrialiser et en faire un système hautement technicisé avec réseau de distribution et alimentation continue.[6] A partir de 1879 les premières lampes à incandescence sont fabriquées en série à New York. Et Thomas Edison de prédire: «Nous allons

2833/99
Design Tiffany
2 x 75 Watt
H 52 cm, Ø 40 cm

Die neue Abhängigkeit von der Zentralversorgung und die ungewöhnliche Lichtstärke von Gas- und Elektrolampen verunsicherten das damalige Publikum. Der Gestaltung von Leuchten kam die Aufgabe zu, über die industrielle Herkunft dieser Lichtmaschinen hinwegzutäuschen. Noch nach dem Anschluß der Haushalte ans Stromnetz entzündete man Öllampen und Kerzen im Wohnzimmer, um sich mit diesem autarken Licht von der Zentralversorgung zu distanzieren. Zur Milderung der Helligkeit wurden kleine Stoffvorhänge über die Lichtquellen gestülpt. »Der Lampenschirm wurde zu einer Art Karosserie, unter der die notwendige, aber häßliche Maschinerie dem Blick entzogen wurde.«[8] Je leistungsfähiger die Birnen wurden, desto mehr verdunkelten sich die Schirme. Das hatte auch, wie der Kulturhistoriker Wolfgang Schivelbusch feststellt, eine interessante Entsprechung in der Gestaltung der Fenster und Gardinen. Gleich doppelt versuchte man, sich der Zwangsvergesellschaftung zu widersetzen: Der Vorhang sollte das Eindringen der Öffentlichkeit und der Lampenschirm den Ansturm der Industrie in die Wohnung verhindern oder zumindest mildern.[9] Elektrisches Licht wurde als entauratisierend empfunden, weil es den Raum bis in den letzten Winkel schattenlos erhellte. Lichtgestaltung mußte der homogenen Illumination wieder Atmosphäre geben.
Der Amerikaner Louis Comfort Tiffany war einer der ersten, der diese »Lichtverpackung« zur Blüte entwickelte. Der ausgebildete Maler begann mit Glasmalereien und gestaltete Bleiglasfenster, die so farbenprächtig wie gotische Kirchenfenster waren. Nachdem er 1882 das Weiße Haus in Washington umgestaltet hatte, entwarf er Glasschirme für Lampen, deren Farbenspiel dem ungegenständlichen Kunstlicht wieder scheinbar Körper und fließende Masse gaben. Tiffanys Mosaikkunst verwandelte Lampenschirme in Blütenkelche, in Zauberpilze oder Reptilien. Sie markierte einen Höhepunkt des Jugendstils, jener

with a cable network and continuous energy supply, ready to go into production.[6] From 1879 onwards he commercially produced the first practicable electric lightbulbs in New York and he prophesied: »We shall make electric lighting so cheap that only rich people will be able to afford a candle.«[7]
The new dependency on the centralized supply and the unusual intensity of light produced by gas and electric lamps caused unease among the public of the time. Lamp designers were faced with the task of hiding the industrial origins of these light machines. Even after households had been connected to the electrical grid system, people still lit oil lamps and candles in their living-rooms in an attempt to distance themselves from the central supply with their own self-sufficient systems. In order to subdue the brightness, small cloth shades were used to cover the light source. »The lampshade became a kind of shell under which the necessary but ugly mechanics were hidden from view.«[8]
The more powerful the bulbs, the darker the lampshades became. As the cultural historian Wolfgang Schivelbusch concluded, this had an interesting parallel in the fashioning of windows and curtains. The attempt to resist the socialization process that was being forced on the community was two-fold: the curtain was intended to hinder the penetration of the outside world into the home, while the lampshade was meant to stop, or at least soften the onslaught of industry.[9] Electric light was considered to spoil the atmosphere because it completely lit up the entire room, right down to the smallest corner. Lighting design had to restore the atmosphere to this homogenous illumination.
The American Louis Comfort Tiffany was one of the first to develop this »packaging for lights«. A studied painter, Tiffany began by painting on glass, and designed leaded lights that were as gloriously colourful as

créer une lumière électrique si bon marché que seuls les riches pourront encore se payer une chandelle.»[7]
Le public de l'époque est déconcerté: il se voit dépendre tout à coup d'un organisme central de distribution et face à des lampes à gaz et des lampes électriques d'une intensité lumineuse jamais vue. Il s'agit maintenant de faire oublier l'origine industrielle des lampes en les dotant de formes agréables. Les ménages sont maintenant raccordés au réseau de distribution, mais on allume encore des lampes à huile et des bougies dans le salon pour se distancier de l'organisme central d'alimentation. On pose des petits rideaux autour des sources de lumière pour en adoucir l'intensité. «L'abat-jour devint une sorte de carrosserie, sous laquelle se cachait la machine hideuse mais nécessaire.»[8]
La puissance des ampoules s'amplifie et les abat-jour se font de plus en plus épais. L'historien Wolfgang Schiverbusch constate une correspondance intéressante entre l'éclairage et la forme des fenêtres et des rideaux. On essaie doublement de résister à cette sociabilisation forcée: le rideau doit entraver ou du moins gêner le regard des autres, tout comme l'abat-jour doit, de son côté, empêcher l'industrie de pénétrer dans l'appartement ou du moins adoucir ses effets.[9]
On ressent la cruauté de la lumière électrique éclairant la pièce jusque dans ses moindres recoins sans jouer avec les contours ou faire naître des ombres. La forme des lampes permet de recréer une ambiance dans cet éclairage trop homogène.
L'Américain Louis Comfort Tiffany est l'un des premiers à faire s'épanouir cet «emballage de la lumière». Peintre de formation, il commence avec de la peinture sur verre et crée des vitraux aux couleurs aussi vives que celles des vitraux des églises gothiques. Après avoir redécoré la Maison Blanche en 1882, il conçoit des abat-jour de verre dont les couleurs semblent redonner à la lumière artificielle un corps mouvant. Tiffany maîtrise l'art de la mosaïque et

1776/48
Design Tiffany
40 Watt
H 27 cm, Ø 17,5 cm

ästhetischen Abkehr vom eklektischen Historismus des 19. Jahrhunderts, die auf ein einheitliches Totaldesign nach Naturformen orientiert war. 1905 beschäftigte er in seinen New Yorker Studios zweihundert Handwerker, die immer neue und extravagante Formen und Gläser - bis zum Fraktur- und Lavaglas - erfanden.[10]
Der geometrisierende, abstrakte Naturalismus Tiffanys wird irrtümlich als Bindeglied zur nachfolgenden Ästhetik des Art Déco verstanden. Aber das Design nach dem Ersten Weltkrieg hatte kein Verständnis mehr für Lampenfüße in Frauengestalt oder Lichtschirme in Insektenform. Art Déco war eine erste Reaktion auf das Maschinenzeitalter. Mit harten, stakkatierenden Silhouetten, geometrisierenden Ornamenten und kräftigen Primärfarben übernahmen Lampen und Möbel Elemente der Malerei von Picasso und Braque sowie der Jazzmusik in die Inneneinrichtung. Die Entdeckung des Grabes von Tut-Ench-Amun im Jahre 1922 löste eine große Ägypten-Mode aus. Daraus entstand eine merkwürdige Mischung aus zugleich archaischen und stromlinienförmigen Gebilden – Astral-Lampions, Altar-Tischlampen und leuchtende Wolkenkratzer-Stelen –, die von Künstlern wie Edgar Brandt, René Lalique, Maurius Ernest Sabino oder Pierre Chareau stammten.
Die Moderne wollte anfangs Handwerk und Industrie vereinen. Aber das Bauhaus, das während seines Bestehens von 1919 bis 1933 nur 1250 Studenten und 35 Vollzeit-Lehrkräfte hatte, wurde zur einflußreichsten Brutstätte des internationalen Maschinendesigns. Es verwandelte den Traum von der Einheit der Künste in die Industrialisierung von Kunst und Architektur. Bei aller Begeisterung für die neuen Produktivkräfte hatte das Bauhaus einen empfindlichen blinden Fleck: Von Licht und Beleuchtung verstanden seine Vertreter nicht viel. Der englische Designkritiker Reyner Banham hat ausführlich über dieses Defizit der Moderne gespottet.[11] Die Versuche der Bauhaus-Künstler, das nackte, industri-

Gothic church windows. After he had redesigned the interior of the White House in Washington in 1882, he created glass lampshades whose play of colours appeared to restore body and flowing mass to abstract, artificial light. Tiffany's mosaic art transformed lampshades into calyxes, enchanted mushrooms or reptiles. His work marked one culminating point of Art Nouveau, the aesthetic rejection of the eclectic historicism of the nineteenth century in favour of a uniform design based exclusively on natural forms. But Tiffany's contemporaries already considered him too commercial. In 1905 he employed two hundred craftsmen in his studios in New York who were continually inventing new and more extravagant forms of glass, including glass fragments and floated glass.[10]
Tiffany's geometrical, abstract naturalism is wrongly regarded as the link to the aesthetics of the Art Déco movement which followed. But after the First World War lampstands shaped as women or lampshades in the form of insects no longer had a place in modern design. Art Déco was a first reaction to the machine age. With their hard, sharp silhouettes, geometrically shaped ornamentation and strong primary colours, lamps and furniture brought elements of Picasso's and Braque's painting, as well as jazz music into interior design. In 1922 the discovery of the tomb of Tutanchamun prompted an Egyptian vogue which resulted in a singular mixture of creations both archaic and streamlined in design - astral lanterns, altar lamps and skyscraper steles created by artists such as Edgar Brandt, René Lalique, Maurius Ernest Sabino or Pierre Chareau.
Modernism began as a reform movement moulded by various representatives such as the Belgian co-founder of the Bauhaus Henry van der Velde, the Austrian Secession artist Josef Hoffmann and the AEG architect Peter Behrens. The initial aim was to unite craft and industry. But it was the

transforme les abat-jour en corolles, en champignons magiques ou en reptiles. Il marque de son empreinte un des points culminants de l'Art nouveau, qui s'éloigne du style éclectique cher au 19ème siècle et s'oriente sur un design total et homogène inspiré de formes naturelles. En 1905 ses studios de New York emploient deux cents artisans qui créent des formes toujours plus extravagantes et de nouvelles sortes de verres, jusqu'au verre craquelé et au verre volcanique. [10]
On considère le naturalisme géométrisant et stylisant de Tiffany comme un trait d'union entre l'Art nouveau et l'Art déco qui le suivit, mais la vérité est qu'après la Première Guerre mondiale on n'a plus le sens des pieds de lampe en forme de corps féminin ou des abat-jour en forme d'insectes. L'Art déco est l'une des premières réactions à l'ère mécanique. Il est caractérisé par des formes géométriques, des lignes brisées, des volumes simples et de puissantes couleurs primaires; les lampes et les meubles adoptent des éléments de la peinture de Picasso et de Braque ainsi que les éléments du jazz. La découverte du tombeau de Toutankhamon en 1922 déclenche une grande vague égyptienne. Il en résulte un mélange bizarre de formes archaïques et en même temps aérodynamiques: des lanternes vénitiennes, des lampes d'autel et de lumineuses stèles en forme de gratte-ciel créées par des artistes tels que Edgard Brandt, René Lalique, Maurius Ernst Sabino ou Pierre Chareau.
Au départ le style moderne est un mouvement réformateur marqué par des représentants de tendances très diverses qui veut réunir l'artisanat et l'industrie, mais le Bauhaus, qui n'a durant son existence, de 1919 à 1933, que 1250 étudiants et 35 professeurs à plein temps, devient le foyer le plus influent du design industriel. Et tout en rêvant de l'unité des arts, les membres du Bauhaus vont pratiquement industrialiser l'art et l'architecture.
Le Bauhaus admire les nouvelles puissances industrielles et productives, mais

CHAREAU LAMP
Design 1924
Nußbaum, Alabaster, Metall
Walnut, alabaster, metal
Noyer, albâtre, métal

elle Licht unverhüllt zu verwenden, war sowohl Teil ihrer Industriebegeisterung als auch ihrer Unfähigkeit, mit künstlichen Lichtwirkungen zu arbeiten. Für sein eigenes Chefbüro im Bauhaus hatte Walter Gropius zunächst eine konstruktivistische nackte, mobile-artige Deckenlampe aus Röhren vorgesehen, die einem Entwurf des Holländers Gerrit Rietveld nachempfunden war. Doch weil sie zu stark blendete, stellte Gropius später die berühmte Halbkugel-Mattglaslampe seines Bauhaus-Schülers Wilhelm Wagenfeld auf.[12]

Bei den Leuchtenentwürfen des Bauhauses fällt auf, daß häufig Leuchtstoffröhren verwendet werden. Wolfgang Schivelbusch sieht das Aufkommen dieses Rohr-Designs im Zusammenhang mit der damaligen Vorliebe für dynamische, lineare, stabförmige Elemente wie der Rohrpost oder dem Stahlrohrmöbel. In der Ära der Neuen Sachlichkeit entstanden fast ausschließlich Arbeitslampen, die das Wohnzimmer ebenso grell erleuchteten wie das Großraumbüro oder die Fabrik. Abhilfe wollte der Schweizer Kunsthistoriker Sigfried Giedion schaffen. Er war nicht nur wichtigster Theoretiker der Moderne, sondern auch begeisterter Unternehmer. Von 1931 bis 1935 entwickelte er als Hauptaktionär der Schweizer Möbelfirma »Wohnbedarf« das Programm der »indi«-Lampen. Es waren Lampen, die nicht mit Stoffschirmen verhüllt waren, sondern umgedrehte Reflektoren hatten, um das Licht indirekt an die Wand oder die Decke abzustrahlen. Sie sollten die Räume zwar ebenso hell wie die Bauhaus-Lampen erleuchten, aber blendungs- und schattenfrei sein, um ein Maximum an freier, ungebundener Bewegung im Raum zu ermöglichen.[13] Indirektes, helles, diffundierendes Licht kennzeichnet seitdem einen Großteil der modernen Leuchtenentwürfe einerseits und der modernen Architekturästhetik andererseits, die beide zur totalen Übersichtlichkeit bis hin zur Homogenisierung des Raumes tendierten. Diese modernistische Totalbeleuchtung steht in schärfstem Gegensatz

Bauhaus, which during its existence from 1919 to 1939 had only 1250 students and 35 full-time teachers, that became the most influential hotbed of international machine design and transformed the dream of the unity of the arts into the industrialization of art and architecture. With all its enthusiasm for new productive forces the Bauhaus had one sensitive blind spot: its members did not know much about light and lighting. The English design critic Reyner Banham has scoffed at this deficit at length.[11] Attempts by the Bauhaus to make conspicuous use of naked, industrial lighting were as much due to their love of industrialization as to their inability to work with artificial lighting effects. For his own office in the Bauhaus, Walter Gropius had at first intended to use a stark constructivist mobile-like ceiling light made of tubes and based on a design by the Dutchman Gerrit Rietveld. But because the light was too strong Gropius soon installed the famous hemispherical frosted glass lamp of his Bauhaus pupil Wilhelm Wagenfeld.[12]

The frequent use of fluorescent tubes is striking in the lamps designed by the Bauhaus. Wolfgang Schivelbusch sees a connection between the rise of this kind of tubular design and the contemporary taste for dynamic, linear, pipe-like elements such as those of the pneumatic dispatch systems or tubular steel furniture. The age of »Neue Sachlichkeit« (»New Functionalism«) almost exlusively produced work lamps which lit living rooms as brightly as open-plan offices or factories. The Swiss art historian Siegfried Giedion sought to remedy this problem. He was not only the most important theorist of modernism, but also an enthusiastic industrialist. Between 1931 and 1935 he was the main shareholder of the Swiss furniture company »Wohnbedarf« and developed the programme »indi-Lampen« (»indi-lamps«). These lamps were not covered with fabric lampshades; instead they had reversed reflectors that bounced light onto the wall or

ses représentants ne comprennent pas grand chose à la lumière et à l'éclairage, et c'est leur point faible. Le critique de design anglais, Reyner Banham, a raillé par le menu ce déficit du mouvement moderne.[11] Les artistes du Bauhaus tentent d'utiliser la lumière industrielle nue sans l'«emballer» parce que l'industrie les passionne, mais aussi parce qu'ils sont incapables de maîtriser les effets de l'éclairage artificiel. Pour son propre bureau du Bauhaus, Walter Gropius prévoit tout d'abord un plafonnier en tubes, un genre de mobile dépouillé à la manière constructiviste, inspiré d'un projet du Hollandais Gerrit Rietveld. Mais il éblouit trop, et Gropius le remplace par la célèbre lampe hémisphérique en verre mat de Wilhelm Wagenfeld, élève au Bauhaus.[12] Si on étudie les lampes du Bauhaus, on remarque l'utilisation fréquente de tubes fluorescents. Wolfgang Schivelbusch explique que ce design tubulaire est au goût du jour: on préfère les éléments dynamiques, linéaires, en forme de barreau, c'est l'époque des tubes pneumatiques et des meubles en tubes. Au nom de la Nouvelle Objectivité on crée surtout des lampes éclairant les salons de manière aussi crue que les lampes de bureaux ou d'usine. L'historien d'art suisse Sigfried Giedion veut mettre un terme à cela. Il n'est pas seulement le plus important théoricien du mouvement moderne mais aussi un homme d'affaires engagé. De 1931 à 1935 il élabore, en tant qu'actionnaire principal de la fabrique de meubles suisse «Wohnbedarf», le programme des «Lampes indi». Ces lampes n'ont pas d'abat-jour en tissu mais des réflecteurs retournés qui renvoient la lumière sur le mur ou le plafond. Elles doivent éclairer les pièces aussi bien que les lampes du Bauhaus mais sans éblouir et sans créer d'ombres, ceci pour permettre un maximum de mouvement libre dans la pièce.[13] La lumière indirecte, claire et diffuse, caractérise depuis une grande partie des projets modernes aussi bien en ce qui concerne la création de lampes que l'architecture. Dans les

RIETVELD LAMP
Design Gerrit Rietveld 1920
Tecta
3 x 40 Watt
H 155 cm, B 40 cm, D 40 cm
Acrylglas, Holz
Acrylic glass, wood
Verre acrylique, bois

zur heutigen Zerstreuung des Lichts in Dutzende einzelner Quellen.

In Amerika sorgten die aus dem Nazi-Deutschland geflohenen Bauhäusler für eine weite Verbreitung ihrer utilitaristischen Formensprache. Doch auf dem amerikanischen Designmarkt, der seit dem großen Erfolg von Tiffany heiß umkämpft war, gaben Entwerfer wie Raymond Loewy oder Norman Bel Geddes mit ihrer Stromlinienästhetik den Ton an. Derjenige Designer, der wirklich eine stilistische Verbindung zwischen dem vorangegangenen Naturalismus des Jugendstils und dem Funktionalismus des Bauhauses im Lampendesign schuf, war der wenig bekannte Engländer George Carwardine. Anfang der dreißiger Jahre entwickelte er seine »Anglepoise«-Tischleuchte, die halb dem menschlichen Arm, halb einem Bagger abgeschaut war.[14] Daß sie – leicht modifiziert – bis heute hergestellt wird, dafür hat 1937 der norwegische Gestalter Jac Jacobsen gesorgt. Als er die »Anglepoise«-Lampe zum erstenmal sah, erwarb er sofort das Patent und stellte sie erst in Skandinavien und von 1951 an auch in Amerika her.[15] Unter dem Namen »Luxo L 1« ist sie zur Ikone jeder Studentenbude und jeden Büros geworden.

KÜCHENKUNST UND PLASTIKLOOK

Skandinavien wurde nach dem Zweiten Weltkrieg tonangebend in der Designentwicklung. Poul Henningsen entwarf von 1957 an seine Serie der »PH«-Leuchten, die direktes und indirektes Licht gleichzeitig ausstrahlten und deren Schirme von geometrischen Primärformen bis zu abstrahierten Pflanzenformen reichten, etwa das Modell »Artischocke«. Skandinavische Hängeleuchten, gleichgültig ob von Arne Jacobsen oder Anders Pehrson, lassen sich pauschal als Inbegriff der Küchenleuchte bezeichnen, auch wenn sie für andere Zwecke entworfen wurden. Sie vereinen die ergonomischen Qualitäten einer hellen, blendfreien Lichtführung mit den

ceiling. The lamps were intended to light a room just as brightly as the Bauhaus lamps had done, but without the glare or shadows to enable a maximum amount of free movement in the room.[13] Bright, indirect, diffuse light has since become a feature on the one hand of the majority of modern lamp designs and, on the other, of architectural aesthetics, both of which tended toward absolute clarity or even homogeneity of light in a room. This modernistic total illumination contrasts most sharply with our attempts today to distribute light using dozens of single light sources.

In America the Bauhaus members who had fled from Nazi Germany ensured that their utilitarian use of forms became widespread. However, since Tiffany's great success, the American market had been greatly contested, and now designers such as Raymond Loewy and Norman Bel Geddes with their stream-line aesthetics were the decisive influences. The one lamp designer who had truly created a stylistic link between the naturalism of Art Nouveau that had gone before and the functionalism of the Bauhaus was the little-known Englishman George Carwadine. In the early 'Thirties he developed his Anglepoise desk-lamp, the mechanics of which were based partly on the human arm and partly on the excavator.[14] Thanks to the Norwegian designer Jac Jacobsen, the lamp is still in production today, albeit in a slightly modified form. When he first saw the Anglepoise in 1937 he immediately obtained the patent and began production in Scandinavia. In 1951 production also began in America. Under the name »Luxo L1« the Anglepoise has become the icon of every student's digs and every office.

KITCHEN ART AND PLASTIC LOOK

After World War II Scandinavia set the tone in the development of design. Starting in 1957 Poul Henningsen designed his series of PH lamps, which produce direct and indirect light simultaneously and have lamp-

deux cas, l'objectif est de disposer l'espace de manière globalement perceptible, de «l'homogénéiser» en quelque sorte. Cet éclairage total prôné par le mouvement moderne est complètement opposé à la tendance actuelle qui veille à diffuser la lumière à l'aide de nombreuses sources orientées différemment.

Les membres du Bauhaus ayant quitté l'Allemagne nazie veillent à propager leur langage formel utilitaire. Mais sur le marché américain du design la compétition est dure, et depuis le grand succès de Tiffany, les formes aérodynamiques de stylistes tels que Raymond Loewy ou Norman Bel Geddes donnent le ton. Georg Carwardine, un Anglais peu connu, est le seul à créer réellement un lien stylistique entre le naturalisme de l'Art nouveau et le fonctionnalisme du Bauhaus. Au début des années 30 il conçoit sa lampe de table Anglepoise, inspirée en partie du bras humain, en partie d'une pelleteuse.[14] Le styliste norvégien Jac Jacobsen veille en 1937 à ce que cette lampe, légèrement modifiée, soit fabriquée jusqu'à nos jours. Voyant l'Anglepoise pour la première fois, il en achète aussitôt le brevet, la fait fabriquer d'abord en Scandinavie et à partir de 1951 également en Amérique.[15] Depuis elle trône sous le nom de «Luxo L 1» dans toutes les chambres d'étudiants et les bureaux.

ART CULINAIRE ET LOOK PLASTIQUE

Après la Seconde Guerre mondiale la Scandinavie exerce une influence prépondérante sur l'évolution du design. En 1957 Poul Henningsen crée sa série de lampes PH. La lumière qu'elles émettent est à la fois directe et indirecte, et les formes des abatjour vont du plus parfait géométrisme aux motifs floraux stylisés; le modèle «Artichaut» en est un exemple. Les lampes suspendues scandinaves, qu'elles soient l'œuvre d'Arne Jacobsen ou d'Anders Pehrson, sont devenues les lampes de cuisine par excellence, même si elles ont été

ANGLEPOISE
Design Herbert Terry 1933
Anglepoise Lighting Ltd. / Tecta
H max 71 cm
Metall, metal, métal

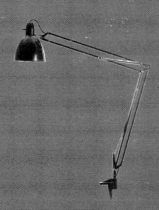

LUXO L1
Design Jac Jacobsen 1937
Jac Jacobsen AS
60 Watt, E 27
H max. 105 cm, ø 16 cm
Metall, Aluminium
Metal, aluminum
Métal, aluminium

ARKITEKT
Ikea of Sweden
60 Watt
H 70 cm, ø 18 cm
Metall, Kunststoff
Metal, plastic
Métal, plastique

Gemütlichkeitswerten sanft modulierter Farben, die oft aus den verwendeten Holz- und Papierstoffen der Schirme resultieren. Anklänge der Skandinavier an japanische Nachkriegsentwürfe sind nicht zu übersehen, etwa an Isamu Noguchis inzwischen weltberühmten China-Lampion namens »Akari« von 1952, der die Leichtigkeit und Flüchtigkeit des Lichts einfängt. Noguchis zusammenlegbare Lichtkugel war jahrelang die Standardleuchte des modernen Schlafzimmers, obwohl – oder vielleicht gerade weil – ihre klinisch weiße und zugleich diffuse Abstrahlung jede Sinnesregung abtötet.

Mit der Einführung des Werkstoffes Plastik ins Industriedesign wußten Ende der fünfziger Jahre die Italiener am besten umzugehen. 1959 hatte der junge Flugzeugingenieur Ernesto Gismondi in Mailand die Lampenfirma »Artemide« gegründet und den jungen Architekten Vico Magistretti angeworben. In seinen Entwürfen – vor allem den Halbkugeln »Mania« und »Eclisse« aus transluzentem Kunststoff – verschmolzen wegen der Modellierbarkeit des Plastiks Halterung und Schirm zu einer Einheit. Die Firma Artemide ist der wichtigste Urheber des heute weltweit verbreiteten Geometrie-Looks im Lampendesign. Zur Entwurfsphilosophie sagt der Firmengründer, seine Lampen sollten auch im ausgeschalteten Zustand schön sein. Was ihn von früheren Leuchtenbauern, etwa Tiffany, unterscheidet, ist die Konstruktionstiefe: Gismondi läßt nicht nur Schirme und Karosserien, sondern die gesamte Leuchte mitsamt der Technik entwerfen und bauen.[16]

Die Brücke zu den wilden sechziger Jahren schlugen die Brüder Achille und Piero Giacomo Castiglioni. Sie schufen 1962 den ersten Ableger einer neuen Kunst der Lichtskulpturen, indem sie einen Autoscheinwerfer an eine Angelrute hängten und damit die neofunktionalistische »Toio«-Leuchte erfunden hatten. Der Entwurf vereinte das dekorative Element mit dem industriell-praktischen. Der dritte der Castiglioni-Brüder, Livio, trieb die Spielerei

shades of various shapes ranging from basic geometric forms to abstract plant forms such as the Artichoke model. Scandinavian suspended lamps, be they Arne Jacobsen's or Anders Pehrson's models, can generally be called the epitome of kitchen lighting, even if they were originally designed for a different purpose. They combine the ergonomic qualities of bright, glare-free lighting with the homeliness of gentle colour modulations, an effect often resulting from the wood and paper used for the lampshades.

Scandinavian designs are distinctly reminiscent of post-war Japanese models such as Isamo Noguchi's now world-famous Chinese lantern, Akari, designed in 1952, which captures the ease and fleeting character of light. Naguchi's foldable ball of light was the standard light in the modern bedroom for years although – or maybe because – its clinically white and yet diffuse light puts an end to any sensual arousals. It was the Italians who knew best how to handle plastic when it was introduced into industrial design in the late 1950s. In 1959 the young aircraft designer Ernesto Gismondi started the lamp company »Artemide« in Milan and took on the young architect Vico Magistretti. In his designs Magistretti took advantage of the mouldability of plastic, allowing the mounting and the lampshade to merge into one. Famous examples are the hemispherical Mania and Eclisse lamps made of translucent plastic. The company »Artemide« is the most significant creator of the geometric look in lamp design, which has now become widespread across the world. With reference to his design philosophy, the company founder said that his lights should look good even when they are switched off. The main point in which Gismondi differed from earlier lamp-makers such as Tiffany is the depth of his construction: Gismondi not only has lampshades and stands made, but he has the whole light, including its mechanics, designed and contructed.[16]

It was the two brothers Achille and Piero

conçues à d'autres fins. Elle allient les qualités ergonomiques d'un éclairage clair, non éblouissant, aux qualités de confort et d'ambiance de leurs couleurs doucement modulées, résultant souvent des tissages de bois ou de papier des abat-jour. Impossible d'ignorer chez les Scandinaves les réminiscences de projets japonais d'après-guerre, par exemple la lanterne chinoise Akari créée par Isamu Noguchi en 1952 et devenue mondialement célèbre entretemps: elle capture la légèreté et la fugacité de la lumière. La sphère pliable de Noguchi a été pendant des années la lampe standard de la chambre à coucher moderne, bien que - mais peut-être faudrait-il dire «parce que» - sa lumière froide et diffuse tue tout élan sensuel.

A la fin des années 50 le plastique fait son apparition et les Italiens s'avèrent maîtres dans l'art d'exploiter ses possibilités. En 1955 le jeune ingénieur en aéronautique Ernesto Gismondi fonde à Milan l'usine de lampes «Artemide» et engage le jeune architecte Vico Magistretti. Le plastique est si aisément modelable que dans ses projets, surtout les hémisphères Mania et Eclisse en plastique translucide, le support et l'abat-jour se confondent. La maison Artemide est à l'origine du design géométrique aujourd'hui répandu dans le monde entier. Interrogé sur la philosophie de l'entreprise, son créateur répond que ses lampes doivent être aussi belles éteintes qu'allumées. Ce qui distingue Gismondi des constructeurs antérieurs, par exemple Tiffany, est la profondeur de la construction: les abat-jour et «les carrosseries» sont conçus et construits ici, mais aussi la lampe globale, technique incluse.[16]

Les frères Achille et Piero Giacomo Castiglioni jettent les ponts jusqu'aux années 60. En 1962 ils créent les premiers objets lumineux en suspendant un phare de voiture à une canne à pêche, ce qui donne la première lampe néo-fonctionnaliste Toio. Elle joint l'élément décoratif à l'élément industriel et pratique. Livio, le troisième des frères Castiglioni va plus loin encore en in-

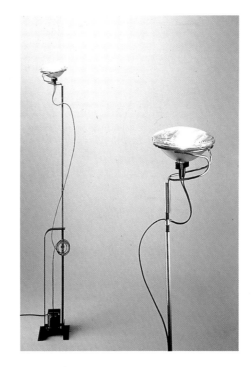

TOIO
Design Achille and Piero Giacomo Castiglioni
1962
Flos S.p.a.
300 Watt
H max. 200 cm
Stahl, Messing, vernickelt
Steel, nickel-plated brass
Acier, laiton nickelé

Autoscheinwerfer und Angelrute:
neofunktionalistischer Designklassiker
Car headlight and fishing-rod: a classic
example of neo-functionalist design
Phare de voiture et canne à pêche:
Un classique du design néo-fonctionnaliste

noch weiter und zog 1969 eine Weihnachtsbaum-Glühlampenkette durch einen durchsichtigen Plastikschlauch. Das war die erste verformbare Leuchte namens »Boalum«, die sich sogar knoten ließ. Kunststoffleuchten von Joe Colombo oder die berühmte hängende »Aalreuse« von Bruno Munari (Modell »Falkland« von 1964, eine Art ausgeleierter China-Lampion) trieben die formalen Spielereien bis zur Ermüdung weiter.

Das Aufkommen von Lichtschienensystemen in den sechziger Jahren steht in direktem Zusammenhang mit der damaligen Begeisterung für Technik und Massenproduktion. Serialität, Reihung und Standardisierung wurden nicht nur zu industriellen, sondern auch zu künstlerischen Formprinzipien. Einheitlichkeit der Rahmenbedingungen bei Flexibilität im Detail, eine Art technischer Strukturalismus, kennzeichnet vor allem die von der Lüdenscheider Firma Erco seit den sechziger Jahren entwickelten Lichtschienensysteme.[17]

1981 rief der Architekt und Designer Ettore Sottsass auf der Mailänder Möbelmesse die Memphis-Bewegung ins Leben. Das war der Beginn der »Postmoderne« im Design. Anstelle der ergonomisch-verspielten Spätmoderne schufen die Gestalter eine sinnliche, farbensprühende und abstrakt-archaisierende Formensprache. Leuchten wurden in die Möbel eingebaut oder in Totem-Skulpturen eingepackt, wodurch die Lichtquellen sekundär wurden.

NOSTALGIE DES TECHNISCHEN

Man sagt heute, die dritte industrielle Revolution, die Computerisierung, sei zugleich die erste großtechnische Umwälzung gewesen, die im Kinderzimmer begann. Ohne Video-Spiele, Joy-Stick und Commodore-PC wäre der Siegeszug der Computer wohl kaum derart triumphal gewesen. Doch auch die vorangegangene zweite industrielle Revolution der Elektrifizierung hatte, wie bereits dargestellt, zunächst außerhalb der industriellen Sphä-

Castiglioni who bridged the gap across to the raving 'Sixties. In 1962 they created a new form of light sculpture when they hung a car headlight onto a fishing rod and thus invented the neofunctionalist Toio-light. The design combined decorative and practical industrial elements. In 1969 the third Castiglioni brother, Livio, took the game one step further when he pulled a set of Christmas tree lights through a clear plastic tube. This became the first shapable light, called Boalum, which could even be tied in knots. The synthetic lights of Joe Colombo or the famous suspended Aalreuse designed by Bruno Munari (the Falkland model of 1964, a kind of overstretched Chinese lantern)took the fun and games with form to their limit.

The rise of light track systems in the 1960s is directly connected to the enthusiasm of the time for technology and mass production. Production in series and standardization became the principles of form on the industrial as well as the artistic level. They also became the directives in all areas of art, ranging from fashion and music to the design of mega-structures by avant-garde architects (and led to the depressing mass housing schemes of the time, among other things). A uniform framework with a flexibility of detail combined to become characteristic of a kind of technical structuralism. This technical structuralism became the hallmark of the light-track systems produced by the Lüdenscheid-based company Erco. The systems were developed during the 1960s and used mainly in industry.[17]

In 1981 the architect and designer Ettore Sottsass brought the Memphis movement into being at the furniture fair in Milan. This marked the beginning of post-modernism in design. Instead of the playful ergonomics

troduisant une guirlande de Noël électrique dans un tuyau de plastique transparent. Il crée Boalum, la première lampe déformable dans laquelle on peut même faire un nœud. Les lampes en plastique de Joë Colombo ou Aalreuse, la célèbre lampe à suspension de Bruno Munari (Modèle Falkland de 1964, une sorte de lampion chinois usé, sont d'autres exemples de ces exercices formels traités jusqu'à l'épuisement.

Il faut voir l'apparition de systèmes d'éclairage sur rails après 1960 dans le contexte d'une époque éprise de technique et de fabrication en série. Le classement en séries et la standardisation deviennent des principes industriels mais aussi artistiques. Les systèmes d'éclairage sur rails créés par la maison Erco de Lüdenscheid et surtout utilisés dans l'industrie se caractérisent par une recherche de l'unité de l'ensemble et de la flexibilité dans le détail, un genre de structuralisme technique.[17]

En 1981 Ettore Sottsass, architecte et designer, fonde pendant le Salon du Meuble de Milan le mouvement Memphis qui représente le début du «post-moderne» au niveau du design. Les concepteurs remplacent le genre moderne tardif, ergonomique et ludique, par des formes sensuelles, des couleurs vives, un style archaïque stylisé. Les lampes sont intégrées dans les meubles ou emballées dans des sculptures-totems, les sources de lumière passant ainsi complètement à l'arrière-plan.

NOSTALGIE DE L'ÈRE TECHNIQUE

Il paraît que la troisième révolution industrielle, l'ère informatique, est le seul bouleversement technique à grande échelle qui ait commencé dans les chambres d'enfants. Le triomphe de l'ordinateur n'aurait certes pas été aussi complet si les jeux vidéo, le joy-stick et le PC Commodore n'avaient pas existé. Pourtant la révolution industrielle précédente, celle de l'électrification, a, nous l'avons vu, débuté elle aussi hors du domaine industriel. Ce ne sont pas

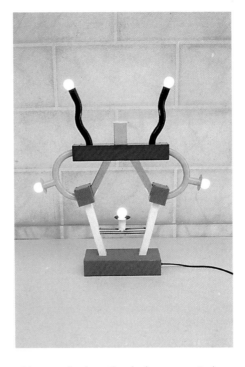

ASHOKA
Design Aldo Cibic, Cesare Ongaro 1981
Memphis
50 Watt + 5 x 40 Watt
H 220 cm, B 52 cm, D 39 cm
Porzellan, Aluminium, mehrfarbig
Porcelain, aluminum, multicoloured
Porcelaine, aluminium, polychrome

re begonnen. Die Gewöhnung an den elektrischen Strom geschah nicht durch die Maschinen, Turbinen und Fließbandstraßen der großen Industrie, sondern durch das elektrische Licht. Die Massennachfrage nach Strom wurde erst ausschießlich durch die Beleuchtungen im Haushalt und auf der Straße stimuliert, bevor später die ersten industriellen Abnehmer ans Netz kamen. Daß etwas so Harmloses wie diese kleinen Glaskugeln mit Kohlefädchen das Leitfossil der bislang bedeutendsten großtechnischen Umwälzung sind, kann man sich heute kaum mehr vorstellen. Seit einigen Jahren scheinen sich die Designer wieder daran zu erinnern, wie stark die Symbolkraft des Lichts ist. Seit der Verbreitung der Halogentechnik in den siebziger Jahren versuchen sie deshalb, den Verbrauchern ein ganzes Bündel an Botschaften mitzuverkaufen, die sie in Rohform niemals loswürden. Wer heute sein Licht einschaltet, setzt nicht mehr Glühlampen in Gang, sondern Beleuchtungskörper mit Blendschutzklappen, UV-Absorbern, Wabenlinsen, Glasfarbfiltern und Kaltlichtreflektoren, in denen wahlweise Leuchtstoffröhren, Halogenmetalldampflampen oder Natriumdampfhochdrucklichter als Downlight-Systeme glühen. In den Wohnzimmern herrscht die totale technische Mobilmachung, die bis zur Niedervoltbefeuerung für das Nachttischchen reicht. Derselbe Joe Colombo, der in den sechziger Jahren seine dekorativ leuchtenden Plastikschüsseln entworfen hatte, heizte auch diese Technisierung mit seinen spindeldürren Stehleuchten in Form von Satellitenantennen an. Achille Castiglioni zitierte die euklidische Geometrie, als er 1972 seine Schreibtischlampe »Ipotenusa« als schrägen Stab entwarf, der im Verhältnis zur Tischplatte die Hypotenuse eines rechtwinkligen Dreiecks beschreibt. Und Mario Bellini gestaltete seine »Eclipse«-System-Strahler wie eine Kreuzung aus Kamera und Bühnenscheinwerfer.

Die Lichtrevolution der Halogenstrahler ist der Automobil- und Bühnentechnik zu ver-

of late modernism, the designers created a sensuous, multi-coloured and abstractly archaic use of forms. Lights were built into furniture or disguised as totem sculptures, whereby the light source itself was of merely secondary importance.

NOSTALGIA OF TECHNOLOGY

The third industrial revolution, computerization, is nowadays said to be the first great technical revolution to have begun in the playroom. Without video or joy-stick games and without the Commodore PC, the triumphal march of computers would not have been anything like as spectacular as it was. The preceding industrial revolution, that of electrification, had, as we have seen, also originated outside the realms of industry. It was not through the machines, turbines, and conveyor-belt production lines of mass industry that people grew accustomed to electricity, but through electric light. The humble light-bulb was the catalyst for world-wide electrification. The mass demand for electricity first arose exclusively from the need for lighting in the home and on streets, well before industrial consumers were connected to the network. Nowadays one can hardly imagine how something as insignificant as these small glass balls containing carbon fibres could become the index fossil of the most significant technical revolution yet. For some years now designers seem to have been remembering how great the symbolic value of light is. Since the spread of halogen technology in the late 1970s they have therefore tried to sell the consumer a whole lot of messages which they would not have been able to pass on in their original form. Nowadays, when we switch a

les machines, les turbines et les chaînes de fabrication de la grande industrie qui ont familiarisé les gens avec l'électricité, mais la lumière de leurs salons. L'électricité éclaire les maisons et les rues bien avant que les premiers clients industriels ne soient rattachés au réseau.

Que ces anodines petites boules de verre munies d'un filament de carbone soient le point de départ du bouleversement industriel le plus important jusqu'à ce jour est difficile à concevoir aujourd'hui. Depuis quelques années les designers semblent se remémorer la puissance symbolique de la lumière. Et depuis l'apparition de l'éclairage halogène dans les années 70 ils essaient pour cette raison de vendre aux consommateurs avec la lampe tout un paquet de messages qu'ils n'arriveraient jamais à écouler sous leur forme brute. Aujourd'hui on n'allume plus une ampoule, on fait fonctionner des corps lumineux dotés de volets antiéblouissants, d'absorbeurs de rayons ultraviolets, de lentilles alvéolées, d'écrans de verre coloré et de réflecteurs à lumière froide dans lesquels luisent au choix des tubes incandescents, des lampes halogènes à vapeur métallique ou des lampes à vapeur de sodium à haute pression. Toute la technique moderne est mobilisée dans les salons, et même dans la lampe basse tension qui orne la table de chevet.

Joë Colombo, celui qui a conçu les lampes-bassins de plastique des années 60, accélère également cette emprise de la technique avec ses lampadaires filiformes ressemblant à des antennes de satellite. Achille Castiglioni retrouve les principes de la géométrie euclidienne lorsqu'il conçoit en 1972 sa lampe de bureau Ipotenusa, une baguette oblique, qui décrit l'hypoténuse d'un triangle rectangle dont la base serait la surface du bureau. Et Eclipse, le système d'éclairage de Mario Bellini, est un mélange de caméra et de projecteur de théâtre.

L'industrie automobile et les techniques de l'éclairage de scène nous ont valu l'apparition révolutionnaire des lampes halogènes

IPOTENUSA
Design Achille Castiglioni 1976
Flos S.p.a.
50 Watt
H 55 cm, B 60 cm
Metall, Acrylglas
Metal, acrylic glass
Métal, verre acrylique

danken. Im Licht der Halogenstrahler leuchten die Wohnungen heute wie Landstraßen oder Illusionsräume auf. Die erste erfolgreiche Halogentischlampe, Richard Sappers »Tizio« von 1970, entwickelte den Baggergreifarm von Jacobsen weiter zu einer freien Pendelmechanik. Dort schwebte das Halogenlämpchen zum erstenmal scheinbar schwerelos über die Köpfe hinweg. Manche Betrachter fühlten sich bei diesem Entwurf auch an Ölbohrpumpen in Kalifornien erinnert.

Seit dem Siegeszug der Halogentechnik sehen moderne Leuchten aus wie technische Armaturen beim Zahnarzt oder wie die Schnürboden-Mechanik eines Theaters. Doch die Mode der Geometrie-Leuchten strahlt heute weniger den Technik-Terror der sechziger Jahre, sondern nur noch pure Nostalgie aus. Genauso wie bei der High-Tech-Architektur handelt es sich um die romantische Beschwörung einer verflossenen Zeit, als die große Industrie noch blühte und die klassische Mechanik noch nicht vom Medienzeitalter ausgehebelt war. In den konstruktivistischen Baggerarmen, Kränen, Winkeln und Lichtpfeilen auf den Schreibtischen steckt eine gewaltige Sehnsucht nach Ruhe und Ordnung.

Die Geschichte des elektrischen Lichts ist heute die fortwährende Miniaturisierung und Entmaterialisierung der Beleuchtungskörper. Das gibt den Designern eine gewaltige Gestaltungsfreiheit, die aber oft in merkwürdige Licht-Zelebrationen ausufert. Ihren vorläufigen Höhepunkt hat diese Entwicklung mit den von den Brüdern Castiglioni bereits in den siebziger Jahren aufgegriffenen Niedervoltsystemen erreicht, die der Schweizer Hannes Wettstein weiterentwickelte und die der Deutsche Ingo Maurer perfektionierte. Wie die Oberleitungen von Eisenbahnen spannen sich die Drähte durch die Wohnzimmer, an denen sich die lustigen Lämpchen wie Efeu entlangranken. Durch bloßes Berühren lassen sie sich einschalten und dimmen. Solche Fingerspitzen-Lichtmagie suggeriert, daß der Strom direkt aus dem Äther genom-

light on, we are not simply setting an electric light-bulb aglow; we are using anti-glare shutters, UV-absorbers, honeycomb anti-dazzle screens, glass colour filters and cold beam reflectors behind which fluorescent tubes, metal halide lamps or sodium vapour lamps are illuminated as downlight systems. Absolute technical mobilization dominates in our homes, right down to low-voltage lighting for our bedside tables. The same Joe Colombo who had designed decorative illuminated plastic bowls in the 'Sixties also stimulated this mechanisation with his spindly standard lamps designed in the shape of satellite antennae. Achille Castiglione cited Euclidean geometry when he designed his desk-light Ipotenusa in 1972; it consisted of a diagonally positioned rod which represented the hypotenuse of a right-angled triangle whose base was the desk top. Mario Bellini designed his Eclipse system light to look like a cross between a camera and a stage light.

It is the car industry we have to thank for the revolution of the halogen lamp. Halogen lamps light up homes like country roads or imaginative spaces. In 1970 Richard Sapper designed the first successful halogen table lamp, Tizio, a further development of Jacobsen's excavator arm, to a free pendant mechanism. The small halogen bulb appeared to float weightlessly above people's heads. The design reminded some of the pumps on Californian oil fields.

Since the victory of halogen technology, modern lamps have begun to look like the technical instruments one might see at the dentist's or like the stage mechanics of the theatre. Yet nowadays the fashion for geometric lights has less of the technological terror of the 'Sixties; it is purely of nostalgic value. Just as with high-tech architecture, lights conjure up a romantic image of past times when there was a great industrial boom and classical mechanics had not been forced to give way to the age of the mass media. The constructivist excavator arms, cranes, angles and illuminated rods

qui éclairent aujourd'hui nos appartements devenus ainsi routes ou pièces imaginaires. «Tizio» de Richard Sapper, la première lampe halogène de bureau à connaître le succès en 1970, reprend le bras de l'excavatrice de Jacobsen mais le transforme en un mécanisme à balancier libre. C'est la première fois que la petite lampe halogène plane au-dessus des têtes. Certains la comparent aux pompes des puits de pétrole californiens.

Ces lampes halogènes semblent sorties tout droit d'un cabinet de dentiste ou du cintre d'un théâtre. Mais elles n'ont plus aujourd'hui cette allure si technique, caractéristique des années 60, elles sont au contraire pure nostalgie. Semblables en cela à l'architecture high-tech, elles évoquent de manière romantique une époque où la grande industrie fleurissait et où la diffusion massive de l'information n'avait pas encore supplanté les mécaniques classiques. Dans ces bras d'excavatrice, ces grues, ces angles et ces flèches de lumière se fait jour une violente nostalgie du calme et de l'ordre.

Aujourd'hui on assiste à une miniaturisation et une dématérialisation continue des corps lumineux. Les designers peuvent s'exprimer très librement, ce qui déborde souvent en de bizarres célébrations de la lumière. Provisoirement à la pointe du progrès, le système de lampes à basse tension, déjà conçu par les frères Castiglioni pendant les années 70, développé ensuite par le Suisse Hannes Wettstein et perfectionné par l'Allemand Ingo Maurer est entré dans les salles de séjour. Les câbles d'acier se tendent au-dessus des têtes comme les fils aériens des chemins de fer et les drôles de petites lampes corolles s'y accrochent. Elles s'allument ou changent d'intensité lorsqu'on les touche. Ce contact digital magique suggère que l'électricité vient directement des espaces infinis et non de la centrale nucléaire la plus proche. Le macramé halogène de ces funiculaires à basse tension fournit, exactement comme l'ampoule archaïque d'Edison, cinq pour

TIZIO 35
Design Richard Sapper 1990
Artemide
35 Watt
H 95 cm, L max. 90 cm
Metall und Kunstharz
Metal, synthetic resin
Métal et résine synthétique

men wird und nicht aus dem Atomkraftwerk stammt.

Das Halogen-Makramee der Niedervolt-Seilbahnen erzeugt genau wie Edisons archaische Glühbirne nur fünf Prozent Licht und 95 Prozent Wärme. Der Einsparungseffekt ist mehr ein optischer durch Materialverschlankung. Die Energievergeudung ist fast gleich geblieben. Zwar ist die Lichtausbeute mit der Verkleinerung der Birnen erheblich gestiegen, ebenso deren Haltbarkeit; aber im Endeffekt beträgt die absolute Stromersparnis gegenüber herkömmlichen Glühlampen gerade acht Prozent. Und für die geniale Augenwischerei mit den Niedervolt-Systemen, die so sparsam aussehen, daß alle Stromspar-Appelle an ihnen abgleiten, zahlt das Publikum bereitwillig das Zwanzigfache einer herkömmlichen Birne – ganz zu schweigen von dem Sondermüll in den Trafokästchen, in denen pfundweise teure Metallrohstoffe versteckt sind, die später in den Müllverbrennungsanlagen verdampfen. Wer weiß schon, daß er weder Leuchtstoffröhren, Halogenlampen noch Trafos in den Mülleimer werfen darf, sondern sie getrennt als Sondermüll entsorgen muß?

Der herkömmlichen nackten Glühbirne, jenem Meisterwerk der industriellen Arte povera, hatte der Schrifsteller Thomas Pynchon einst sogar ein literarisches Denkmal gesetzt, als er die mit Bewußtsein begabte Glühbirne namens Byron erfand, die gegen die gefräßige Industrie kämpfen mußte.[18] Im 19. Jahrhundert konnte sich noch niemand darüber hinwegtäuschen, wie kostbar und lebensgefährlich zugleich der Strom ist. Daß dies heute zunehmend verdrängt wird, zeigt schon der Formenwandel der Lichtschalter. Die ersten Drehhebel ragten unförmig wie Telefonglocken aus der Wand. Auch später, als die großen, umständlich zu bedienenden Flügel- und Wippschalter aufkamen, steckte in deren mechanischer Unbeholfenheit noch unfreiwillig eine Ehrfurcht vor der wundersamen Lichterzeugung. Absurderweise gab es noch bis in die Nachkriegszeit Drehschalter

on writing-desks are the expression of a great yearning for peace and order.

The history of electric light is nowadays the continuing miniaturization and dematerialization of light sources. This leaves designers great freedom, which, however often escalates to produce the strangest celebrations of light. The first climax was reached in the 'Seventies when the Castiglioni brothers began work on low-voltage systems, which were further developed by the Swiss Hannes Wettstein and perfected by the German Ingo Maurer. Two wires are suspended across the room just like the overhead cables of a train, and the whimsical little lights are entwined along them like creeping ivy. A single touch is enough to switch them on or dim them. Such delicate magic could almost lead one to believe that the energy comes from the ether and not from a nearby nuclear power station. The low-voltage cable construction of this halogen macramé produces only 5% light and 95% heat, just as Edison's original light-bulb had done. The economical effect is more an optical one due to the sleek design. The amount of energy wasted remains about the same. Admittedly the small bulbs emit considerably more light and are much longer-lasting, but in actual fact only 8% less energy is used by halogen bulbs than by conventional bulbs. The low voltage system appears so economical that it is immune to all appeals to save energy, and the public willingly pay twenty times as much for this ingenious trickery as for the conventional light-bulb – not to mention the many pounds of precious metal inside the transformer, which should be treated as special waste but which will later vaporize in the incinerators at the waste disposal plant. How many people actually realize that they should not throw fluorescent tubes, halogen bulbs or transformers into their normal household waste, but that these should be disposed of as special waste?

With Byron, the intellectual light bulb who had to fight against the greed of industry,

cent de lumière et quatre-vingt-quinze pour cent de chaleur. Le matériel, plus fin, donne l'impression de faire des économies, mais le gaspillage énergétique reste presque aussi important. Le rendement, tout comme la résistance, a considérablement augmenté avec la miniaturisation des ampoules, mais, en fin de compte, l'économie réelle de courant par rapport aux ampoules normales ne s'élève qu'à huit pour cent. Et le public paie sans broncher vingt fois le prix d'une ampoule normale pour ces systèmes à basse tension qui éveillent l'illusion d'être économiques et que les consommateurs utilisent en toute bonne foi. On oublie aussi de mentionner les nombreux métaux bruts très chers qui se cachent dans les transformateurs et finiront dans les centres d'incinération, alors qu'il s'agit de déchets à traiter spécialement. Les tubes incandescents, les lampes halogènes et les transformateurs ne doivent pas être jetés à la poubelle, mais la plupart des gens l'ignorent.

L'écrivain Thomas Pynchon a immortalisé l'ampoule nue commune, ce chef-d'oeuvre de l'Arte povera industriel, en créant «Byron», la lampe à incandescence douée de conscience et partant en guerre contre l'industrie et ses appétits démesurés.[18] Au 19e siècle tout le monde sait combien l'électricité est précieuse et, en même temps, dangereuse. Rien que la forme des commutateurs nous montre combien on essaie de refouler cette idée aujourd'hui. Les premiers leviers tournants et disgracieux sortent du mur comme les anciens téléphones. Même plus tard lorsque les grands commutateurs en aile ou à poussoir, difficiles à manipuler, font leur apparition, il y a dans ces mécanismes maladroits un respect involontaire de la lumière miraculeuse. On trouve encore après la guerre des commutateurs rotatifs pour la lumière, héritage absurde du mécanisme à réglage continu de la mèche ou de la flamme des lampes à huile et à gaz.

Aujourd'hui les commutateurs plats, carrés, aux coins arrondis disparaissent

für das Licht, die überflüssigerweise das Erbe des stufenlosen Docht- und Flammenmechanismus von Öl- und Gaslaternen mitschleppten.

Heute sind die flachen Lichtschalter mit ihrer Quadratform und den abgerundeten Ecken völlig in die Wand zurückgetreten. Man bedient sie beiläufig im Vorübergehen mit der flachen Hand, dem Ellbogen, der Schulter oder gar mit dem Kinn. In der Achtlosigkeit dieser Bewegung steckt en miniature das gesamte Dilemma heutiger Energieverschwendung. Immerhin werden in der Bundesrepublik Deutschland heute acht Prozent des gesamten elektrischen Energiebedarfs für Beleuchtungen eingesetzt, wovon einiges einzusparen wäre.[19]

DIE SCHATTEN DES LICHTS

Ein Gestaltungselement taucht in der Beleuchtung der Privatsphäre heute immer wieder auf: die Lichtdramaturgie der Ausstellungs- und Schaufensterbeleuchtungen. Die Akzentstrahler und Spotlights im heutigen Wohnzimmer sind Hervorbringungen der Kaufhaus-Welt. Zur pointierten Präsentation der Waren müssen dort bestimmte Objekte hervorgehoben und andere ausgeblendet werden. Es ist paradoxerweise ein ebenso illuminierendes wie verdunkelndes Licht, das nicht mehr bloß Helligkeit ausstrahlt, sondern zugleich Schatten produziert. »Man braucht viel Licht, um einen Raum dunkel zu kriegen«, sagt der Erco-Leuchtenfabrikant Klaus-Jürgen Maak über die Kunst, das funktionale zum dekorativen Licht und den Nutzraum zum Erlebnisraum zu machen.[20] Der amerikanische Lichtgestalter Claude Engle, der mit Norman Foster die Hongkong und Shanghai Banking Corporation eingerichtet hatte, meint: »Jeder kann einen ganzen Raum mit Licht füllen; das Geheimnis liegt darin, die Dunkelheit richtig zu gebrauchen.«[21] Nicht mehr Gardine und Lampenschirme, sondern die Führung und Modellierung des Lichts selbst bestimmen die Raumwirkung. Früher dominierte der zentrale festliche

the writer Thomas Pynchon once paid a literary tribute to that masterpiece of arte povera, the humble light-bulb. In the nineteenth century nobody could be under any illusion about how valuable and yet how dangerous electricity is. The changing shape of light switches shows how this realization is being suppressed today. The first turning knob protruded from the wall as clumsily as did contemporary telephone bells. Later, too, when the awkward dolly and rocker switches became widespread, their impractical mechanics still embodied a deep respect for the wondrous production of light. Absurd as it may seem, rotary switches were used well into the post-war period, superfluous allusion to the legacy of the stepless wick and flame mechanism of oil and gas lanterns.

Nowadays the slim light switches with their square shape and rounded corners have receded so far as to almost become part of the wall. They are switched on and off casually in passing and using the open hand, the elbow, the shoulder or even the chin. The entire dilemma of modern energy wastage is epitomized in this thoughtless movement. After all, in the Federal Republic of Germany 8% of all energy is used for lighting, much of which could be saved.

THE SHADOW OF LIGHT

One particular element of design crops up continually in domestic lighting nowadays: the dramaturgy of exhibition and shop-window lighting. Accent spots and spotlights in modern living-rooms originated in the world of the department store. In order to present goods certain objects must be emphasized and others must be cut out. Paradoxically, a light that is just as illuminating as it is darkening causes not only light, but also shadows. »You need a lot of light to make a room dark,« says the lamp manufacturer Klaus-Jürgen Maak of Erco about the art of making functional light decorative, and utilized space into a space to be experienced.[20] The American lighting ex-

complètement dans les murs. On les enfonce en passant avec la paume de la main, le coude, l'épaule et même le menton. Cette nonchalance n'est qu'un pâle reflet de notre attitude actuelle face au gaspillage de l'énergie. En Allemagne aujourd'hui le pourcentage de la consommation d'électricité destinée à l'éclairage s'élève à huit pour cent,[19] et il serait possible de baisser ce chiffre.

LA LUMIÈRE ET SES OMBRES

On note que l'habitat a récupéré les effets décoratifs et dramatisants utilisés dans l'éclairage des expositions et des vitrines. Les projecteurs à faisceau concentré et les spotlights que l'on trouve dans les salles de séjour actuelles sortent du monde des grands magasins. Pour présenter les produits de manière soutenue, il faut mettre en valeur certains objets en en faisant disparaître d'autres. On utilise paradoxalement une lumière qui éclaire autant qu'elle obscurcit, qui ne produit plus seulement de la clarté mais des ombres. «Il faut beaucoup de lumière pour obscurcir une pièce» dit Klaus-Jürgen Maak, fabricant des lampes Erco, interrogé sur l'art de transformer la lumière fonctionnelle en lumière décorative et l'espace utilitaire en un antre mystérieux.[20] Le designer de lampes américain Claude Engle qui a décoré avec Norman Foster la Hongkong and Shanghai Banking Corporation, déclare, quant à lui:«Tout le monde peut remplir un espace de lumière; le secret, c'est de bien utiliser l'obscurité.»[21] Fini le temps des rideaux et des abat-jour, c'est la lumière elle-même, modulée, qui crée l'ambiance. Le salon aristocratique était dominé par un lustre majestueux, que l'on retrouve d'ailleurs dans la croix de bois à cinq branches ornée de lampes de porcelaine des foyers bourgeois. Jusqu'ici on a toujours centralisé la lumière; même dans les constructions neuves les prises sont installées au milieu des plafonds. Mais dans la décoration intérieure les designers et les utilisateurs s'effor-

Kronleuchter den Salon, der später im bürgerlichen Heim als fünfarmiges Holzkreuz mit Porzellanhauben fortlebte. Das diffuse Licht ist bis heute zentralisiert. Selbst in Neubauten werden immer noch die unsinnigen Deckenanschlüsse in der Zimmermitte installiert. Doch in der Innenarchitektur bemühen sich Designer und Benutzer, die Lichtquellen zu vervielfachen und zu dezentralisieren. Aber zugleich wird der Strahl einer jeden Lichtquelle gebündelt. Die multiplen Steh-, Hänge-, Spreiz-, Klemmlampen und Lichtleisten tauchen in jedem Winkel des Raumes auf, erhellen aber jeweils nur kleine Ausschnitte. Gegenüber dem unsensiblen, homogenisierenden Milchlicht der Moderne werden einzelne Objekte aus dem Raum gleichsam herausgeschnitten. In dem mit Punktstrahlern und Wall-Washern dramatisierten Wohnzimmer taucht das Bild des Verkaufsraumes wieder auf, den die Waren nur scheinbar verlassen haben. Die Dominanz der Objekte, etwa der Audio-Video-Geräte, ist heute im Wohnzimmer genauso groß wie im Hi-Fi-Studio. Die Konsumgüter kehren in der Privatsphäre zudem viel massierter wieder, weil sie nicht mehr in ihrer Vielheit gleichgültig nebeneinander aufgereiht sind wie im Laden, sondern sich weitaus stärker als Einzelstücke in den Vordergrund schieben. Die Schatten und Kontrastwirkungen heutiger Bau- und Beleuchtungsformen sind zu einer eigenständigen Gestaltungskunst geworden. Ob man mit Licht den Raum kultisch mystifizieren, meditativ beruhigen, theatralisch dramatisieren oder in ihm den Reiz der kommerziellen Warenpräsentation auskosten will, das kann angesichts der in diesem Buch ausgewählten Leuchten jeder selbst entscheiden.

pert Claude Engle, who worked together with Norman Foster on the Hong Kong and Shanghai Banking Corporation, said, »Anyone can fill an entire room with light; the secret lies in the ability to make proper use of darkness.« [21] It is no longer curtains and lampshades but the arrangement and moulding of light that determine the effect of a room.

In the past the splendid central chandelier dominated the room. It lived on later in the bourgeois home as a five-armed wooden construction with porcelain covers. Diffuse light is still centralised today; even in new buildings unnecessary electrical points are installed into the middle of the ceiling, yet interior designers and users are attempting to use multiple, decentralised light sources. At the same time, however, the beams of each source remain bundled. The many lamps, be they standard, suspended, splayed, clamp or strip lights, appear in every corner of the room, but each illuminates only a small area of the room. Contrary to the insensitive, homogeneously distributed milky light used by modernist designers, these lamps pinpoint single objects in the room.

The dramatization of living-rooms with spotlights and wall-washers conjures up images of a shop from which the goods only appear to have gone. The dominance of objects such as audio and video apparatus is equally as important in living-rooms as in hi-fi studios. The appearance of consumer goods has more impact in a domestic environment because they are no longer lined up indifferently in masses, as in a shop, but come to the fore more strongly as individual objects. The shadows and contrasting effects of modern buildings and lighting have become an art-form in their own right. With the help of the lights presented in this book anyone can decide what atmosphere to create in a room, be it one of ritualistic mysticism, meditative peacefulness, theatrical dramatization, or perhaps the enjoyment of the appeal of commercially presented of goods.

cent de multiplier les sources de lumière. En même temps le rayonnement de chaque source de lumière est focalisé. Des lampadaires, des lampes à suspension, des lampes au support à incliner, écarter, visser et des bandes lumineuses apparaissent dans chaque coin de la pièce, mais chacun d'eux n'éclaire qu'une petite partie de celle-ci.

Ce qui les différencie des lampes à lumière laiteuse, uniformisante et peu sensible issues du mouvement moderne est le fait qu'ils attirent l'attention sur certains objets de la pièce.

L'image du grand magasin mettant certains produits en valeur nous revient à l'esprit dans la salle de séjour dramatisée par des spots et des diffuseurs muraux. L'importance des objets, par exemple les appareils audio-vidéo, est aussi grande aujourd'hui dans la salle de séjour que dans le studio hi-fi. De plus les biens de consommation sont plus remarqués dans l'habitation privée où l'objet unique se pousse en avant, que dans le magasin où les appareils les plus divers installés côte à côte éveillent l'indifférence.

Les ombres et les effets contrastés que produisent les bâtiments et éclairages actuels sont le résultat d'un art à part entière. Chacun peut décider à l'aide des lampes présentées dans ce livre s'il veut faire d'un espace le lieu d'un culte mystérieux, un îlot de paix propre à la méditation, la scène dramatique d'un théâtre ou une salle d'exposition au charme bien commercial.

1 Hans Sedlmayr, Das Licht in seinen künstlerischen
  Manifestationen. Mäander Kunstverlag, Mittenwald
  1978, S. 13 f.
2 Walter Benjamin, Denkbilder, in: Gesammelte Schriften IV, 1. Werkausgabe Band 10. Suhrkamp-Verlag,
  Frankfurt 1980, S. 373
3 Gerhard Auer, Ahnung und Planung. Zum Licht-Be-
  wußtsein des Architekten, in: Ingeborg Flagge (Hg.),
  Licht-Architektur. Karl Krämer Verlag, Stuttgart und
  Zürich 1991, S. 127 ff.
4 ders., S. 133
5 Wolfgang Schivelbusch, Lichtblicke. Carl Hanser Verlag, München und Wien 1983, S. 22 ff.
6 Das Grundlagenwerk der Technikgeschichte der Elektrifizierung ist: Thomas P: Hughes, Networks of
  Power. Electrification in Western Society 1880 -
  1930. John Hopkins University Press, Baltimore
  1983. Das Buch begründet auch eine neue Theorie
  der Technikgeschichtsschreibung, indem es nicht
  mehr Einzelerfindungen, sondern großtechnische Sy-
  stemzusammenhänge untersucht.
7 zit. nach: Jeremy Myerson, Lamps and Lighting. Conran Design Guides, London 1990, S. 7
8 Schivelbusch, a. a. O., S. 167
9 ders., S. 178
10 Barty Phillips, The Christopher Wray Book of Decorative Lighting. Webb & Bower Publishers, Exeter,
  1987, S. 22-25
11 In der Einleitung zu »The Architectur of the Well-tem-
  pered Environment« spottet Reyner Banham über die
  große Technik- und Designgeschichte »Die Herrschaft der Mechanisierung« von Sigfried Giedion, in
  der die Frage der Beleuchtung völlig ignoriert worden
  ist. Siehe dazu Stanislaus von Moos, Nachwort zu
  Sigfried Giedions »Die Herrschaft der Mechanisierung«. Europäische Verlagsanstalt, Frankfurt 1982, S.
  790
12 Wolfgang Schivelbusch, Licht, Schein und Wahn. Verlag Ernst & Sohn, Berlin 1992, S. 101 ff.
13 Stanislaus von Moos, Nachwort zu Sigfried Giedions
  »Die Herrschaft der Mechanisierung«. Op.cit.,
  S. 784 ff.
14 Jeremy Myerson, Lamps and Lighting, a. a. O., S. 16
15 Die Zuschreibung der »Anglepoise«-Leuchte, dem
  Vorgänger der »Luxo L 1«, ist umstritten. Im Hand-
  buch »Moderne Klassiker« (Verlag Gruner & Jahr,
  Hamburg, o. J., S. 98 f.) werden als ihre Erfinder
  O. C. White und Herbert Terry genannt.
16 Interview mit Ernesto Gismondi in: Raum und Wohnen, Nr. 5/1988, S. 63-68
17 Das Industriethema der Lichtsysteme sprengt den
  Rahmen dieses auf das Interiordesign konzentrierten
  Buches bei weitem. Weiterführende Informationen
  enthält beispielsweise das Buch: Erco Lichtfabrik,
  Verlag Ernst & Sohn, Berlin 1990.
18 Thomas Pynchon, Die Enden der Parabel. Rowohlt-
  Verlag, Reinbek 1989
19 Angaben des Zentralverbandes der Elektrotechnik-
  und Elektronikindustrie, Bonn
20 zit. nach: »Der Raum wird zur Leuchte - Die Revolution in der Innenarchitektur«, in: Der Spiegel, Nr.
  12/1987, S. 255 - 265
21 zit. nach: »Wo Licht ist, ist auch Schatten«, in: Neue
  Zürcher Zeitung, 2. Dezember 1989

1 Hans Sedlmayer, Das Licht in seinen künstlerischen
  Manifestationen, Mäander Kunstverlag, Mittenwald
  1978, pp. 13 ff.
2 Walter Benjamin, Denkbilder, Gesammelte Schriften
  IV.1., Werkausgabe vol. 10, Suhrkamp, Frankfurt
  1980, p.373
3. Gerhard Auer, »Ahnung und Planung. Zum Licht-
  Bewußtsein des Architekten«, Licht-Architekten,
  Ingeborg Flagge (ed.), Karl Krämer Verlag, Stuttgart
  and Zürich 1991, pp. 127 ff.
4 ibid., p.133
5 Wolfgang Schivelbusch, Lichtblicke, Carl Hanser
  Verlag, Munich and Vienna 1983, p. 22 on.
6 A basic study of the technological history of electrification is Thomas P. Hughes, Networks of Power.
  Electrification in Western Society 1880-1930, John
  Hopkins University Press, Baltimore 1983. The book
  also puts forward a new theory of technological histo-
  riography which no longer examines single inven-
  tions, but major technical systems.
7 Jeremy Myerson, Lamps and Lighting. Conran
  Design Guides, London 1990, p.7
8 Schivelbusch, op. cit., p. 167
9 ibid., p. 178
10 Barty Phillips, The Christopher Wray Book of Decorative Lighting, Webb & Bower, Exeter 1987, pp. 22-25
11 In the introduction to »The Architecture of the Well-
  Tempered Environment« Reyner Banham mocks
  Sigfried Giedion's broad history of technology and design titled »Die Herrschaft der Mechanisierung«, in
  which the question of lighting is totally ignored. See:
  Stanislaus von Moos, epilogue to Sigfried Giedion's
  »Die Herrschaft der Mechanisierung«, Europäische
  Verlagsanstalt, Frankfurt 1982, p. 790
12 Wolfgang Schivelbusch, Licht, Schein und Wahn,
  Ernst & Sohn, Berlin 1992, p. 101 on.
13 Stanislaus von Moos, epilogue to Sigfried Giedion's
  »Die Herrschaft der Mechanisierung«, op. cit.,
  p. 784 on
14 Jeremy Myerson, Lamps and Lighting, op. cit.,
  p. 16
15 There are contrasting opinions on the invention of the
  Anglepoise, the forerunner of Luxo L 1. In the hand-
  book »Modern Classics« (Gruner & Jahr, Hamburg,
  n.d., p. 98 on), O. C. White and Herbert Terry are
  named as the inventors.
16 Interview with Ernesto Gismondi, Raum und
  Wohnen, No. 5/1988, pp. 63-68
17 The industrial aspect of lighting systems is beyond
  the scope of this book about interior design. Further
  information can be found, for example, in the book
  Erco Lighting Factory, Ernst & Sohn, Berlin 1990.
18 Thomas Pynchon, Die Enden der Parabel, Rohwolt,
  Reinbek 1989
19 Figures quoted by the Zentralverband der Elektro-
  technik- und Elektroindustrie, Bonn.
20 »Der Raum wird zur Leuchte - Die Revolution in der
  Innenarchitektur«, Speigel, no. 12/1987, pp. 255-265
21 »Wo Licht ist, ist auch Schatten«, Neue Zürcher
  Zeitung, 2.12.89

1 Hans Sedlmayr, Das Licht in seinen künstlerischen
  Manifestationen, Mäander Kunstverlag, Mittenwald
  1978, p. 13 suiv.
2 Walter Benjamin, Symboles, in: Gesammelte Schriften IV.1., vol. 10, Suhrkamp-Verlag, Francfort 1980,
  p. 373
3 Gerhard Auer, «Ahnung und Planung. Zum Licht-Be-
  wußtsein des Architekten», in: Ingeborg Flagge (Ed.),
  Licht-Architektur, Karl Krämer Verlag, Stuttgart et
  Zurich 1991, pp. 127 suiv.
4 ibid., p. 133
5 Wolfgang Schivelbusch, Lichtblicke. Carl Hanser
  Verlag, Munich et Vienne 1983, pp. 22 suiv.
6 Thomas P. Hughes, Networks of Power. Electrification in Western Society 1880 - 1930. John Hopkins
  University Press, Baltimore 1983. C'est l'ouvrage de
  base sur l'histoire de la technique de l'électrification.
  Il établit également une nouvelle théorie de l'écriture
  de l'histoire de la technique, en ce qu'il analyse les
  rapports mutuels des systèmes techniques à l'échelle industrielle et non plus les découvertes en détail.
7 Cité d'après: Jeremy Myerson, Lamps and Lighting.
  Conran Design Guides, Londres 1990, p. 7
8 Schivelbusch, op. cit. p. 167
9 ibid., p. 178
10 Barty Philips, The Christopher Wray Book of Decorative Lighting. Webb & Bower Publishers, Exeter
  1987, pp. 22 - 25
11 Reyner Banham, dans son introduction à «The Architectur of the Welltempered Environment», se moque
  de la grande histoire de la technique et du design
  «Die Herrschaft der Mechanisierung» de Sigfried
  Giedion qui ignore complètement la question de
  l'éclairage. Voir à ce sujet Stanislaus von Moos,
  postface à Sigfried Giedion «Die Herrschaft der
  Mechanisierung». Européische Verlagsanstalt,
  Francfort 1982, p. 790
12 Wolfgang Schivelbusch, Licht, Schein und Wahn.
  Verlag Ernst & Sohn, Berlin 1992, pp. 101 suiv.
13 Stanislaus von Moos, postface à Sigfried Giedion
  «Die Herrschaft der Mechanisierung», cité ci-dessus,
  p. 784 suiv.
14 Jeremy Myerson, Lamps and Lighting, op. cit. p. 16
15 La question de l'attribution de la lampe Anglepoise,
  qui a précédé la lampe Luxo L 1 est controversée. Le
  manuel «Moderne Klassiker» (Verlag Gruner & Jahr,
  Hambourg, n. d., p. 98 suiv.), nomme O. C. White et
  Herbert Terry comme étant ses inventeurs.
16 Interview avec Ernesto Gismondi in: Raum und
  Wohnen, n° 5/1988, pp. 63 - 68
17 Le thème industriel des systèmes d'éclairage dépas-
  se de beaucoup le cadre de ce livre qui se concentre
  sur la décoration d'intérieur. A titre d'exemple le livre
  Erco Lichtfabrik, Verlag Ernst & Sohn, Berlin 1990,
  contient des informations plus détaillées.
18 Thomas Pynchon, Die Enden der Parabel, Rowohlt-
  Verlag, Reinbek 1989
19 Chiffres fournis par l'association centrale de l'industrie de l'électronique et de l'électrotechnique, Bonn
20 Cité d'après: «Der Raum wird zur Leuchte - Die Revolution in der Innenarchitektur»,
  in: Der Spiegel, n° 12/1987, pp. 255 - 265
21 Cité d'après: «Wo Licht ist, ist auch Schatten», in:
  Neue Zürcher Zeitung du 2 décembre 1989

SCHERBENGERICHT
Design Ingo Maurer
Ingo Maurer GmbH

Objekt für Villa am See
Design object for villa beside lake
Objet pour villa au bord d'un lac

STANDARD GLÜHLAMPE

Ein Glühfaden, genannt Wendel, aus Wolf-
ramdraht wird durch den Lampenstrom auf
etwa 2500 Grad Celsius erhitzt. Durch
diese hohe Temperatur gibt die Wendel
sichtbare Strahlung, also Licht, ab. Die Gas-
füllung mit Argon dient dazu, die Verdamp-
fung des Wolframmetalls zu reduzieren. Je
höher die Wendeltemperatur, desto höher
ist die Lichtausbeute, aber um so kürzer ist
auch die Lebensdauer der Birne. Bei Lampen mit einer Kryptonfüllung wird die Lichtausbeute durch deren geringere Wärme-
leitfähigkeit verbessert. Neue Glühbirnen
namens »Linestra« besitzen einen extrem
langen Glaskolben mit gestreckter Wendel.
Sie sehen Leuchtstofflampen zum Ver-
wechseln ähnlich, ergeben jedoch ein viel
weicheres Licht, das zudem dimmbar ist.

THE CONVENTIONAL ELECTRIC LIGHT-BULB

A filament or »coil« made of tungsten is
heated to about 2500 degrees Centigrade
using electricity. This extreme temperature
causes the coil to emit visible beams called
light. The argon gas filling serves to reduce
the vaporization of the tungsten. The hotter
the coil, the more light it emits, but the
shorter the life span of the bulb. In bulbs
containing krypton gas the yield of light is
higher, since the gas filling is not such a
good conductor of heat. A new kind of
light-bulb called Linestra is extremely long
in shape with an extended coil. The bulb is
almost identical in appearance to a fluorescent tube, but it produces a much softer
light which can also be dimmed.

LA LAMPE À INCANDESCENCE

Un filament incandescent de tungstène, dit
spirale, est chauffé jusqu'à 2500 degrés
Celsius par le courant de la lampe. Cette
température fait rayonner le filament, qui
émet de la lumière. L'ampoule est remplie
d'argon, ce qui doit réduire l'évaporation du
tungstène. L'intensité lumineuse est pro-
portionnelle à la température du filament et
plus celle-ci est élevée, plus la vie de l'ampoule est courte. Les ampoules remplies
de krypton produisent moins de chaleur et
plus de lumière. Les nouvelles lampes à incandescence Linestra possèdent une ampoule extrêmement longue et un filament
allongé. Elles ressemblent à s'y méprendre
à des tubes fluorescents, mais la lumière
qu'elles produisent est beaucoup plus
douce et son intensité peut être réglée.

STANDARDGLÜHLAMPE, FASSUNG E 27
AMPOULE STANDARD, DOUILLE E 27
STANDARD LIGHT-BULB, HOLDER E 27

GLOBE, FASSUNG E 27
GLOBE, DOUILLE E 27
GLOBE, HOLDER E 27

REFLEKTOR, FASSUNG E 27
REFLECTEUR, DOUILLE E 27
REFLECTOR, HOLDER E 27

STANDARDGLÜHLAMPE, FASSUNG E 14
AMPOULE STANDARD, DOUILLE E 14
STANDARD LIGHT-BULB, HOLDER E 14

CONCENTRA, FASSUNG E 27
CONCENTRA, DOUILLE E 27
CONCENTRA, HOLDER E 27

REFLEKTOR, FASSUNG E 14
REFLECTEUR, DOUILLE E 14
REFLECTOR, HOLDER E 14

HALOGEN LAMPE

Halogenlampen sind weiterentwickelte miniaturisierte Glühlampen, in denen zusätzlich ein Halogenkreislauf abläuft und die
aus dickerem, temperaturresistentem
Quarzglas hergestellt werden. Die Wolf-
ramwendel wird mit einer um 100 bis 300
Grad höheren Temperatur betrieben als
normale Glühlampen. Dies würde zur Ver-
dampfung des Wolframs führen, das sich
an der Kolbeninnenwand niederschlagen
und das Glas schwärzen würde. Zudem
würde der Glühdraht an seiner schwäch-
sten Stelle durchbrennen. Um dies zu verhindern, werden dem aus Argon und Stick-
stoff bestehenden Füllgas der Lampe Jod
und Brom zugegeben, die zu den Haloge-
nen gehören. Sie verbinden sich mit dem

HALOGEN BULBS

Halogen bulbs are a further developed
miniature version of the conventional light-
bulb, with an additional halogen cycle; they
are made of thicker, heat-resistant quartz
glass. The tungsten coil is heated to a temperature 100 to 300 degrees higher than a
conventional bulb. This would normally
cause the tungsten to vaporize and precip-
itate inside the bulb, thus blackening the
quartz. The filament would also burn out at
its weakest point. To avoid this the halogen
gases iodine and bromine are added to the
argon and nitrogen filling which combine
with the tungsten to form a gaseous com-
pound. The volatile tungsten halides ionize
on the hot filament, thereby continually
renewing it. At the same time iodine and

LA LAMPE HALOGÈNE

Les lampes halogènes sont des lampes à
incandescence de petite taille qui contiennent un halogène et sont fabriquées en
verre dur résistant aux chocs thermiques.
La température atteinte par la spirale de
tungstène est de 100 à 300 degrés Celsius
plus élevée que dans la lampe à incandescence normale. Normalement le tungstène
devrait s'évaporer et se déposer sur les parois de l'ampoule en noircissant le verre,
de son côté le filament métallique devrait
fondre à son endroit le plus fragile. Afin
d'éviter ceci on ajoute au mélange d'argon
et d'azote contenu dans l'ampoule, de
l'iode et du brome qui sont des halogènes.
Ils s'associent au tungstène et forment
une combinaison gazeuse. Les halogénu-

Wolfram und bilden ein gasförmiges Gemisch. Die leichtflüchtigen Wolframhalogenide zersetzen sich wieder am heißen Glühdraht. Letzterer wird auf diese Weise ständig rezykliert. Gleichzeitig werden Jod und Brom frei und beginnen ihren Kreislauf von neuem. Die Halogene fangen also quasi die verdampften Wolframteilchen in der kühleren Außenzone der Lampe chemisch ein und verhindern so die Schwärzung des Glases.

Wegen ihrer UV-Strahlung sollten Designerlampen, die eigentlich nicht für den Einsatz am Schreibtisch gedacht sind, mit Schutzgläsern versehen werden, die achtzig Prozent der UV-Strahlung absorbieren. Gegenüber dem Wärmeverlust der Standard-Glühlampe von 95 Prozent haben Halogenbirnen einen Wärmeverlust von etwa sechzig Prozent, der ungefähr dem erzeugten spektralen Anteil an infrarotem Licht zusammen mit den sehr hohen Temperaturen der Leuchtwendel entsprechen. Die General-Electric-Forschungslabors in Amerika haben einen Filterstoff entwickelt, der nur den sichtbaren Anteil des Lichts durchläßt. Der Infrarot-Anteil wird wieder auf die Leuchtwendel reflektiert und hält deren Temperatur hoch. Dadurch wird die Außentemperatur ebenso wie die Strommenge der Glühbirne reduziert. Diese Lampen sind aber noch nicht auf dem Markt erhältlich.

bromine are set free and the cycle begins again. In short, the halogens capture the tungsten vapour in the cooler parts of the light-bulb and stop them blackening it. Because of their ultra-violet light, designer lamps not intended as desk-lamps should be equipped with protective glass which absorbs 80% of the UV-rays. In comparison to conventional light-bulbs, which have a heat loss of 95%, halogen bulbs lose about 60%, which is approximately equal to the amount of infra-red light in the spectrum plus the extremely high temperatures of the coil. The research laboratories at General Electric in America have developed a filter substance which allows only the visible part of light to pass through. The infra-red is reflected back onto the coil to keep its temperature up. Thus the outside temperature can be reduced, as well as the amount of electicity needed. However, these lamps are not yet on the market.

res de tungstène, très volatils, se décomposent de nouveau sur le filament chaud qui est ainsi sans cesse recyclé. L'iode et le brome sont libérés et recommencent leur circuit. Les halogènes «captent» donc chimiquement les particules de tungstène évaporées dans la zone extérieure moins chaude de la lampe, et empêchent ainsi le verre de noircir.

Les lampes de designer, qui ne sont en fait pas conçues pour être utilisées sur un bureau, devraient être munies de verres de protection absorbant quatre-vingt pour cent des rayons ultraviolets qu'elles produisent. La perte de chaleur des lampes à incandescence normales s'élève à quatre-vingt-quinze pour cent, par contre celle des ampoules halogènes n'est que d'environ soixante pour cent, ce qui correspond à peu près au rayonnement infra-rouge produit avec en plus la chaleur due à la température très élevée de la spirale lumineuse.

Les laboratoires de recherche de la General Electric en Amérique ont conçu un filtre qui laisse uniquement passer la partie visible de la lumière. Le rayonnement infrarouge est renvoyé sur la spirale et la maintient à haute température. Ce procédé réduit la température extérieure et la quantité d'électricité utilisée par l'ampoule. Mais ces lampes ne sont pas encore commercialisées.

HALOGEN, FASSUNG E27
HALOGÈNE, DOUILLE E27
HALOGEN, HOLDER E27

HALOGEN, 12 V
HALOGÈNE, 12 V
HALOGEN, 12 V

R7S HALOGEN, 220V
R7S HALOGÈNE, 220V
R7S HALOGEN, 220V

HALOGEN KALTLICHTSPIEGEL, 12V
MIROIR À LUMIÈRE FROIDE HALOGÈNE, 12V
HALOGEN KALTLICHTSPIEGEL, 12V

LEUCHTSTOFFLAMPEN (ENTLADUNGSLAMPEN)

An den beiden Enden eines Glasrohres sind wendelförmige Wolframelektroden vakuumdicht eingeschmolzen. In diesen sogenannten »Gasentladungslampen«, die im

FLUORESCENT TUBES (DISCHARGE LAMPS)

Coil-shaped tungsten electrodes are soldered in at both ends of a vacuum-sealed glass tube. In these so-called »gas discharge lamps«, which are generally

LAMPES FLUORESCENTES (LAMPES À DÉCHARGE)

On fixe aux deux extrémités d'un tube de verre des électrodes de tungstène en forme de spirale, le tube est alors vide d'air. Dans les «lampes à décharge gazeu-

alltäglichen Sprachgebrauch irrtümlich »Neonlampen« genannt werden, verursacht ein elektrischer Strom, der durch Gas oder Dampf, meist Argon und Quecksilber, geführt wird, die Ionisation der Atome. Diese Ionen sind energetisch nicht stabil, verbinden sich wieder und fallen dadurch auf ein tieferes, stabileres Energieniveau zurück. Die Energie, die bei diesem Vorgang frei wird, tritt in Form von Ultraviolettlicht auf. Dieses kann der Mensch nicht sehen. Die Strahlung wird daher durch Leuchtstoffpulver an der Innenseite der Leuchtstoffröhre in sichtbares Licht umgesetzt. Durch die Auswahl der Pulver bestimmt man die Farbe des Lichts.

wrongly referred to as »neon lamps«, an electrical current is passed through gas or vapour (usually argon or mercury), causing the atoms to ionize. These volatile ions combine again and consequently drop to a lower, more stable level of energy. The energy released during this process becomes ultra-violet light. Ultra-violet is not visible to the human eye and is therefore converted into visible light by the fluorescent powder coating on the inside of the tube. The choice of powders determines the colour of the light.

se» appelées par erreur «tubes au néon», un courant électrique passe dans le gaz ou la vapeur, le plus souvent de l'argon et du mercure, et entraîne l'ionisation des atomes. Ces ions ne sont pas stables, ils se combinent à nouveau et trouvent alors un niveau d'énergie plus bas qu'ils peuvent maintenir. L'énergie est libérée sous forme de rayonnement ultraviolet. Il est normalement invisible pour l'homme, mais une poudre fluorescente placée sur les parois intérieures du tube le transforme en lumière visible. Le choix de la poudre détermine la couleur de la lumière.

CIRCULUX
CIRCULUX
CIRCULUX

LEUCHTSTOFFRÖHRE
LAMPE FLUORESCENTE
FLUORESCENT TUBE

ENERGIESPARLAMPEN

Energiesparlampen werden »Kompakt-Leuchtstofflampen« genannt und arbeiten nach demselben Prinzip wie die obengenannten Entladungslampen. Sie lassen sich in herkömmlichen Schraubfassungen verwenden. Es gibt komplette Energiesparlampen, in deren Schraubsockel ein elektronisches Vorschaltgerät integriert ist, und zweiteilige Systeme, die aus einer Lampe mit Stecksockel und einem Adapter bestehen, der das Vorschaltgerät enthält. Die zweiteiligen Lampen haben den Vorteil, daß das Vorschaltgerät nach dem Erlöschen der Lampe nicht weggeworfen werden muß. Die Adapter halten ungefähr drei- bis fünfmal länger als die Lampen. Kompakt-Leuchtstofflampen halten fünf- bis achtmal länger als eine herkömmliche Glühbirne, die nur etwa tausend Stunden brennt. Auf die gesamte Lebensdauer bezogen lassen sich mit einer 13-Watt-Energiesparlampe, die ungefähr die Helligkeit einer 75-Watt-Glühbirne ausstrahlt, dreihundert Kilowattstunden Strom einsparen. Diese Lampen enthalten allerdings fünf

ENERGY-SAVING LAMPS

Energy-saving lamps are called »compact fluorescent lamps« and work on the same principle as the sodium discharge lamps described above. They can be used in the traditional screw fitting. There are two types of energy-saving lamp: integral energy-saving lamps with electronic starters built into the fitting, and two-part systems consisting of a lamp with pins and a socket, and an adapter containing a starter. The two-part system has the advantage that the starter does not have to be replaced when the tube fails. The adapters last three to five times as long as the lamp. Compact fluorescent lamps last five to eight times as long as conventional light-bulbs, which only burn about a thousand hours. In its lifetime a 13-Watt energy-saving bulb, which is about as bright as a conventional 75-Watt bulb, will burn approximately 300 Kilowatt hours of electricity less in order to produce the same amount of light. However, these bulbs contain 5 milligrams of mercury, which must be disposed of in the special

LAMPES ÉCONOMES EN ÉNERGIE

Les lampes consommant peu d'énergie sont appelées tubes fluo-compacts et fonctionnent selon le même principe que les lampes à décharge citées précédemment. On peut les utiliser dans une douille à vis normale. Elles existent en tant que tubes fluo-compacts complets avec gradateur intégré dans le culot et en système à deux corps comprenant une lampe avec culot à broches et un adaptateur contenant le régulateur de puissance. Les lampes à deux corps sont avantageuses en ceci que le régulateur de puissance ne doit pas être jeté lorsque la lampe est usagée. La durée de vie des adaptateurs est trois à cinq fois plus élevée que celle des lampes.
Les tubes fluo-compacts durent cinq à huit fois plus longtemps que les lampes à incandescence normales, qui ne fonctionnent qu'environ mille heures. On peut économiser trois cents kilowattheures avec une lampe compacte de treize watts qui éclaire autant qu'une lampe incandescente de 75 watts. Mais ces lampes contiennent cinq milligrammes de mercure qui, avec les

Milligramm Quecksilber, das zusammen mit den elektronischen Bauteilen im Sockel nur als Sondermüll entsorgt werden darf.

waste, along with the electronic components in the fitting.

pièces électroniques contenues dans le socle, doit être traité après usage comme un déchet spécial.

PL / DULUX
PL / DULUX
PL / DULUX

ENERGIESPARGLÜHLAMPE, FASSUNG E 27
LAMPE ECONOOME, DOUILLE E27
ENERGY-SAVING LIGHT-BULB, HOLDER E 27

SPEZIALLEUCHTMITTEL

SPECIAL LIGHT SOURCES

LAMPES SPECIALES

LINESTRA
LINESTRA
LINESTRA

METALLDAMPFLAMPE
LAMPE À VAPEUR MÉTALLIQUE
METAL VAPOR LAMP

LICHTBEWERTUNG

Lampen werden immer noch nach Watt klassifiziert und gekauft, der physikalischen Einheit für die Leistungsaufnahme oder den Stromverbrauch. Der eigentlich interessantere Wert für den Lichtstrom, der in Lumen (lm) angegeben wird, hat sich noch nicht durchgesetzt. Er drückt die von einer Lichtquelle ausgehende Strahlungsleistung aus, bewertet mit einer genormten Helligkeitsempfindlichkeit des menschlichen Auges. Um zu wissen, mit welcher Intensität das Licht etwa auf eine Tischplatte fällt, muß man die Beleuchtungsstärke kennen. Sie wird in Lux (lx) gemessen und hat den Wert 1, wenn ein Lumen gleichmäßig auf eine Fläche von einem Quadratmeter trifft. Glühlampen produzieren etwa zwölf Lumen pro Watt, Halogenlampen zwanzig Lumen pro Watt, Leuchtstofflampen fünfzig Lumen pro Watt. Jährlich werden weltweit etwa 1,1 Milliarden herkömmliche Glühbirnen produziert. Jeder deutsche Haushalt hat durchschnittlich 24 Brennstellen und verbraucht jährlich 4,5 Glühbirnen.

MEASUREMENT OF LIGHT

Lights are still bought and classified according to their wattage, the watt being the unit used in physics to measure the amount of electricity used. The amount of light emitted measured in lumens would actually be a more relevant piece of information, but it has not yet caught on. The lumen measures performance of a light source. Measurement occurs using a standardized scale of light sensitivity equivalent to that of the human eye. In order to ascertain the intensity of light falling onto a desk-top, for instance, we must know the strength of the illumination. This is measured in lux (lx). One lux is the measurement when one lumen of light is distributed evenly across a surface of one square metre. Conventional light-bulbs produce about 12 lumen per watt, halogen lamps about 20, and fluorescent lights produce about 50 lumen per watt. Every year about 1.1 thousand million conventional light-bulbs are produced. Every German household has on average 24 electrical points and uses 4.5 bulbs per year.

MESURE DE PUISSANCE DE LA LUMIÈRE

On mesure toujours la puissance des lampes en watts, c'est l'unité de mesure du flux énergétique ou de la consommation. Le lumen, unité de mesure du flux lumineux (symbole lm), bien que plus intéressant, ne s'est pas encore imposé. Il exprime l'intensité d'une source lumineuse, mesurée avec une sensibilité à la lumière normalisée. Pour savoir avec quelle intensité la lumière tombe sur une surface, il faut connaître la puissance de l'éclairement. Il est mesuré en lux (symbole lx): 1 lux équivaut à l'éclairement d'une surface qui reçoit un flux lumineux de 1 lumen par mètre carré. Les lampes à incandescence produisent environ douze lumen par watt, les lampes halogènes vingt, et les lampes fluorescentes cinquante. 1,1 milliards de lampes à incandescence sont fabriquées chaque année. Chaque ménage allemand a en moyenne vingt-quatre prises de contact et utilise chaque année 4,5 ampoules à incandescence.

PENDELLEUCHTEN

PENDANT LIGHTS

LAMPES SUSPENDUES

Die an einem Seil oder Stab herabhängende Pendelleuchte ist einer der gebräuchlichsten Leuchtkörper im Haus. Ihre Urform ist der Kronleuchter, der möglichst große Flächen erhellen mußte und das verschwenderischste, am wenigsten gerichtete Licht spendete. Heute werden Pendelleuchten meist in der Küche oder im Eßzimmer bzw. über der Eßecke verwendet. Sie sind die sichtbarsten und verräterischsten Gegenstände im Raum, weshalb ihrer Auswahl die größte Bedeutung zukommt. In Altbauten mit hohen Decken fügen sich Pendelleuchten besser ein als in niedrige Neubauwohnungen. Die allseitig abstrahlenden Modelle, die genau in der Mitte der Zimmerdecke montiert sind, finden heute immer seltener Zuspruch, obwohl Neubauwohnungen immer noch mit diesem unsinnigen zentralen Kabelanschluß unter der Decke ausgerüstet sind. Für eine stärkere Ausrichtung des Lichts sorgen Reflektoren und Schirme, die den Strahl in einem bestimmten Winkel bündeln. Entweder wird das Licht genau auf den darunterstehenden Tisch konzentriert oder in umgekehrter Richtung mit verdrehtem Reflektor unter die Decke gestrahlt. Es gibt auch gleichzeitig nach oben und unten abstrahlende Leuchten, die nur den Bereich auf Augenhöhe abblenden. Eine der intelligentesten Pendelleuchten-Kombinationen ist Achille Castiglionis Modell »Frisbi« von 1978, die ein direktes Downlight durch einen vorgesetzten matten Schirm dämpft und zugleich noch Reflektionen an die Decke abgibt. Ähnlich versuchen auch andere Leuchtendesigner, die Tyrannei der zentralisierten Pendelleuchte zu brechen.

The pendant light, which hangs from a cable or rod, is the most common sort of light in the home. It originates from the chandelier, which had to illuminate as big an area as possible and was the most wasteful and worst focussed producer of light. Nowadays pendant lights are normally used in the kitchen or the dining-area. They are the most visible and telling objects in a room, which is why this choice of light is of utmost importance. Pendant lights suit old buildings with high ceilings better than modern homes with low ceilings. Models which spread light in all directions and are positioned right in the middle of the ceiling are losing in popularity nowadays, although modern homes are still equipped with the nonsensical electrical point in the centre of the ceiling. Reflectors and screens ensure better focussing of light by catching it and directing it at certain angles. Light is either concentrated exactly onto the table standing below or it is pointed in the opposite direction at the ceiling using inverted refectors. Some lamps also direct light upwards and downwards simultaneously, only screening the light at eye level. One of the most intelligent combination pendant lamps is Achille Castiglione's Frisbi (1978). Its direct downlight is subdued by a matt screen which at the same time reflects light onto the ceiling. Other lamp designers are also trying to combat the tyranny of the central pendant lamp in similar ways.

La lampe suspendue à un cordon ou une baguette est le modèle le plus répandu. Le lustre dont elle est issue devait éclairer la plus grande surface possible et gaspillait ainsi beaucoup de lumière. Aujourd'hui on trouve surtout des lampes suspendues dans la cuisine ou la salle à manger. Elles sont les objets les plus visibles et les plus perfides dans la pièce, il est donc important de bien les choisir. Elles sont mieux adaptées aux plafonds hauts des appartements anciens qu'aux appartements modernes. Les modèles diffusant de la lumière sous tous les angles et placés au milieu du plafond sont de moins en moins demandés, il n'empêche que les appartements modernes sont toujours absurdement équipés de ces prises centrales au plafond. Les réflecteurs et les abat-jour focalisent le rayonnement sous un certain angle, et peuvent mieux orienter le flux lumineux. La lumière est dirigée sur la table placée sous la lampe ou sur le plafond, grâce à un réflecteur retourné. Certains modèles orientent la lumière aussi bien vers le haut que vers le bas et ne laissent non éclairée que la zone située à hauteur des yeux. Frisbi créée par Achille Castiglioni en 1978 est particulièrement bien conçue: un écran mat placé sous la source de lumière adoucit la projection directe vers le bas et renvoie la lumière vers le plafond. D'autres designers essaient ainsi de se dégager des contraintes imposées par ce système de suspension centrale.

BOREA

Design David Palterer 1991
Driade
8 x 50 Watt, 1 x 20 Watt
H 140 cm, ø 50 cm
Glas, Messing
Glass, brass
Verre, laiton

BRICHOT

Design David Palterer 1991
Driade
3 x 50 Watt
H 46 cm, ø 45 cm
Glas, Messing
Glass, brass
Verre, laiton

BARINE

Design David Palterer 1991
Driade
H 45 cm, ø 60 cm
Glas, Kupfer
Glass, copper
Verre, cuivre

GIO PONTI

Design Gio Ponti 1946
Venini S. p. a.
12 x 60 Watt
H 80 cm, ø 90 cm
Glas, glass, verre

Neuinterpretation des klassischen
Kronleuchters unter Verwendung von
Muranoglas

New interpretation of classical
chandelier using Murano glass

Réinterprétation du lustre classique
à l'aide de verre de Murano

FONDA EUROPA

Gabriel Ordeig 1990
Santa & Cole
7 x 25 Watt / 6 x 25 Watt
H 20 cm, B 120 cm / H 20 cm, ø 70 cm
Holz, Metall, Papier
Wood, metal, paper
Bois, métal, papier

Ironische Kombination von Kronleuchter
und kleinbürgerlicher Tütenleuchte

Ironic combination of chandelier and
petty-bourgeois lamps with conical
shades

Synthèse ironique de lustre et de lampe
tronconique d'esprit petit-bourgeois

OH

Design Jörg Zeidler 1992
Tobias Grau
20 – 50 Watt
B 15 cm, ø 5 cm / ø 7 cm
Aluminium, Bronze poliert
Aluminum, bronze, polished
Aluminium, bronze poli

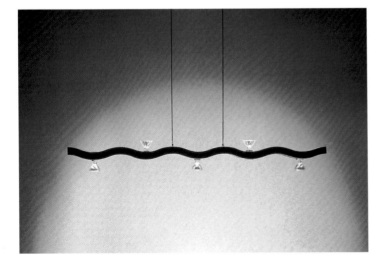

NESSIE

Design Studio De Pas,
D´Urbino, Lomazzi 1989
Stilnovo
5 x 50 Watt
H 100 cm, L 100 cm
Aluminium
Aluminum

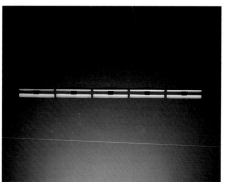

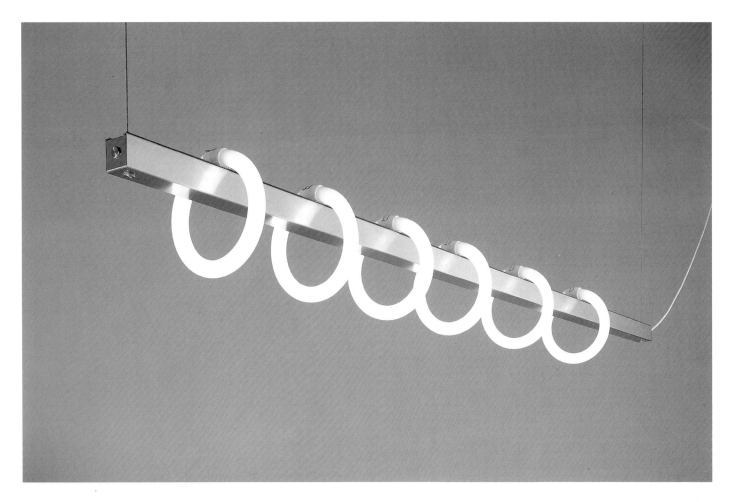

NEON RING LAMP

Design ODIN Design-Team
Odin
6 x 22 Watt
B 220 cm
Gebürsteter Edelstahl
Brushed stainless steel
Acier brossé

Geometrisierende Transformation von Leuchtstofflampen zu einem Lichtobjekt für den Wohnbereich

Fluorescent tube geometrically transformed
into a design object for domestic lighting

Transformation géométrique de lampes
fluorescentes en un objet lumineux pour l'habitat

TAKE FIVE

Design Ginbande 1992
serien Raumleuchten
5 x 35 Watt
L 45 – 160 cm
POM (Kunststoffspritzguß)
POM (plastic injection moulding)
POM (moulage par injection de
matière synthétique)

Horizontal ausziehbare Leuchte nach
dem Prinzip des Scherengitters, stufenlos
von 45 bis 160 cm verstellbar

Uplight, horizontally extendable on the
principle of the concertina barrier,
extendable from 45-160 cm

Lampe linolithe coulissable horizontalement
d'après le principe du grillage à ciseaux,
réglable progressivement de 45 à 100 cm

LAZZURRO

**Design Frans van Nieuwenborg,
Wegmann 1992
Nieuwenborg / Wegmann
58 Watt, 36 Watt
B 150 cm / 120 cm
Kunststoff
Plastic
Matière synthétique**

Futuristischer Lichtpfeil in gespanntem
Bogen, stufenlos höhenverstell- und
dimmbar

Futuristic »arrow« of light in drawn
bow, directly adjustable height and dim-
ming

Flèche de lumière futuriste en arc
tendu, réglable progressivement en
hauteur et en intensité

AIRO

**Design Maurizio Bertoni 1986
Castaldi
36 Watt – 58 Watt
H max. 72,5 cm, B max. 155 cm
Aluminium Druckguß, Stahl
Die-cast aluminium, steel
Aluminum coulé sous pression, acier**

Technizistische Interpretation einer Gelenkarmleuchte aus dem Arbeitsbereich

Technicist interpretation of work-lamp
modelled on jointed arm

Interprétation techniciste d'une lampe
de travail à bras articulé

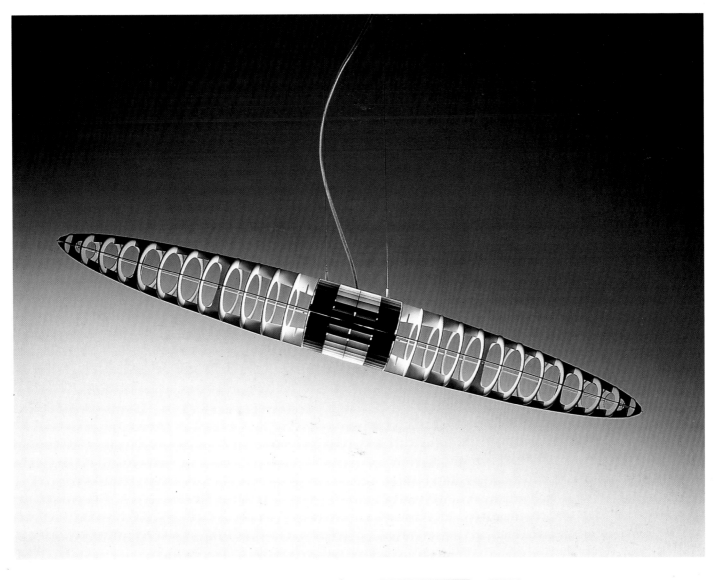

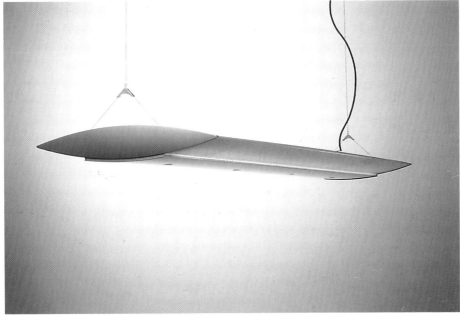

TITANIA

Design Alberto Meda, Paolo Rizzatto 1989
Luceplan
250 Watt
B 70 cm, D 27 cm
Aluminium, aluminum

Schwebende Zeppelinleuchte; auswechselbare
bunte Filter färben das Rastergehäuse

Floating zeppelin light; different coloured filters can be
substituted to give the framework casing its colour

Lampe en forme de dirigeable flottant, des filtres de
couleur amovibles colorent la grille du boîtier

ECONOMY

Design Jürgen Medebach
Belux
4 x TC-I 36 Watt
Metall, metal, métal

Superflache indirekt strahlende Büroarbeitsleuchte,
wahlweise mit einer sensorgesteuerten
Mehrstufenschaltung

Super-flat office lamp, lights indirectly, optional
sensor-controlled variable lighting

Lampe de bureau ultraplate et à rayonnement indirect,
au choix gradateur commandé par palpeur

FRANCESCINA

Design Umberto Riva 1989
Fontana Arte
100 Watt
H 35 cm, ø 17 cm
Glas, Aluminium, Messing
Glass, aluminum, brass
verre, aluminium, laiton

SAVOIE

Design Donato Savoie, Ingo Maurer 1979
Ingo Maurer GmbH
60 Watt
H max. 180 cm
Weißes Porzellan
White porcelain
Porcelaine blanche

BRERA

Design Achille Castiglioni 1992
Flos Arteluce
100 Watt
H 26 cm, B 14 cm
Glas, Kunststoff
Glass, plastic
Verre, matière synthétique

SHADE

Design Sebastian Bergne 1992
Radius
100 Watt
B 36 cm, D 12,5 cm
Stahlblech
Sheet steel
Tôle

Die minimalistische Metallblende
wird direkt auf die Glühbirne gespannt

Minimalist metal shade is pulled
directly over the light-bulb

L'écran de métal minimaliste est
tendu directement sur l'ampoule

EDISON 4

Design Valerio Sacchetti 1989
Sirrah
100 Watt
H 8,5 cm, ø 7 cm
Emailkeramik
Enamel ceramic
Céramique émaillée

LE TRE STREGHE

Design Guenter Leuchtmann 1981
Tecnolumen
100 Watt Halogen
L max. 210 cm, ø 20 cm
Metall, verchromt oder vergoldet
Chromium or gold-plated metal
Métal chromé ou doré

Der Lichtstrahl trifft auf eine massive Glaskugel
und wird diffus und blendfrei nach unten verteilt

Beam hits the solid glass ball and diffuse,
glare-free light is distributed downwards

Le rayon lumineux est intercepté par une boule
de verre massive; il est orienté vers le bas et
éclaire sans éblouir

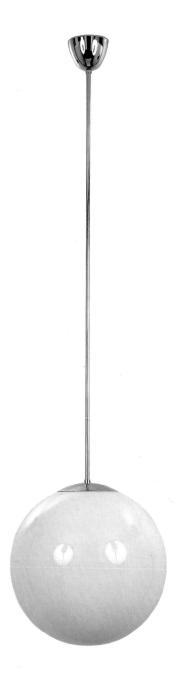

HSF 29

Design anon. 1929
Tecnolumen
2 x 60 Watt
H 110 cm, ø 48 cm
Metall, verchromt
Chromium-plated metal
Métal chromé

HL 99

Design anon. 1900
Tecnolumen
100 Watt
H 120 cm, ø 20 cm / H 125 cm, ø 25 cm
H 130 cm, ø 30 cm / H 135 cm, ø 35 cm
Glas, Metall
Glass, metal
Verre, métal

Gläserne Mondlampe als Weiterentwicklung von
frühmodernen Opalkugeln der Jahrhundertwende

Glass moon-lamp, further development of the early
modern opal balls of the turn of the century

Lampe-lune en verre, perfectionnement des boules
opalines du tournant du siècle

REFLEX

Design Jean-Marc da Costa 1984
serien Raumleuchten
500 Watt, R7s / 70 Watt, RX7s
H 35 cm / 50 cm / 77 cm / 95 cm
Aluminium, Silberfarbe, eloxiert,
oder weiß, pulverbeschichtet
Aluminum, silver finish electrically oxidized,
white finish powder-coated
Aluminium, couleur argentée anodisée
ou recouverte de poudre blanche

URANUS

Boréns AB
TC-L: 3 / 6 x 36 Watt,
QT-DE 12 750 / 1000 Watt
H 110 cm, ø 65 cm / 85 cm
Metall, lackiert
Painted metal
Métal peint

PH 6 1/2

Design Poul Henningsen, Ebbe Christensen,
Sophus Frandsen 1980
Louis Poulsen & Co. GmbH
500 Watt, E40
H 40 cm, ø 65 cm
Aluminium, weiß lackiert
Aluminum, painted white
Aluminium peint en blanc

PH-ZAPFEN

Design Poul Henningsen 1958
Louis Poulsen & Co. GmbH
500 Watt, E40
H 47 cm, ø 60 cm / H 63 cm, ø 72 cm
H 69 cm, ø 84 cm
Aluminium oder Kupfer
Aluminum or copper
Aluminium ou cuivre

Die abstrahierte Pflanzenform führte zu der
gebräuchlichen Bezeichnung »Artischocke«.
Sie strahlt direktes und indirektes Licht
gleichzeitig ab

Because of its abstract plant form this
model became commonly known as »Artichoke«. It produces direct and indirect light
simultaneously.

Le motif végétal stylisé lui a valu le nom
d'«artichaut». Elle éclaire à la fois directement et indirectement

PH-KUGEL-LAMELL

Design Poul Henningsen 1958
Louis Poulsen & Co. GmbH
300 Watt, E 27
H 40 cm, ø 40 cm
Aluminium, weiß lackiert
Aluminum painted white
Aluminium peint en blanc

PX-2077-L72

Design Yamada Shomei
Yamada Shomei Lighting Co.
72 Watt
H 18 cm, B 46 cm, D 46 cm
Holz, Kunststoff
Wood, plastic
Bois, plastique

PX-2041-L102

Design Yamada Shomei
Yamada Shomei Lighting Co.
102 Watt
H 18 cm, B 55 cm, D 55 cm
Holz, Kunststoff
Wood, plastic
Bois, plastique

PX-2043-L102

Design Yamada Shomei
Yamada Shomei Lighting Co.
102 Watt
H 18,5 cm, B 58 cm, D 58 cm
Holz, Kunststoff
Wood, plastic
Bois, plastique

Reduzierte Weiterentwicklung von
archaischen japanischen Papierlampions
als Deckenleuchtenprogramm

The archaic Japanese paper lantern was
further developed and reduced for a
programme of ceiling lights

Perfectionnement en petit format de
lampions japonais archaïques en papier
qui deviennent des plafonniers

DISKOS

Design Giovanni Offredi 1983
Sirrah
16 Watt / 28 Watt
H 8 cm, B 67 cm, ø 60 cm
ABS-Kunststoff, Scheibe mattiertes Vedril
ABS plastic, matt-finish vedril
Plastique ABS, disque en védril mat

NUVOLA SOSPENSIONE

Design Marco Zotta 1991
Bilumen
150 Watt
H 19 cm, ø 20 cm
Sandgestrahltes Glas
Sand-blasted glass
Verre décapé au sable

MIRA

Design Ezio Didone 1990
Flos S.p.a.; koll. Arteluce
200 Watt
H 60 cm, ø 60 cm
Aluminium, Glas
Aluminum, glass
Aluminium, verre

AURORA

Design Perry A. King, Santiago Miranda 1983
Flos S. p. a.
3x 50 Watt, H max. 250 cm, ø 60 cm
Metall, Glas, Kunststoff
Metal, glass, plastic
Métal, verre, plastique

FRISBI

Design Achille Castiglioni 1978
Flos S. p. a.
150 Watt
H 73 cm, ø 60 cm
Metacryl, Metall
Metacryl, metal
Métacryl, métal

Klassische Lösung für eine blendfreie
direkte/indirekte Lichtführung

classical solution for glare-free
direct/indirect lighting

Solution classique pour obtenir une lumière
directe/indirecte non-éblouissante

ZEFFIRO 3

Design Pier Guiseppe Ramella 1987
Flos S. p. a.
150 Watt
H 24 cm, ø 50 cm
Glas, glass, verre

2133

Design Gino Sarfatti 1976
Flos S.p.a. Koll. Arteluce
150 Watt
H max. 240 cm, ø 60 cm
Metall, metal, métal

TRAMA

Design Luciano Balestrini, Paola Longhi 1986
Luceplan
300 Watt
H max. 170 cm + 40 cm, ø 64 cm
Siebdruckpolycarbonat, Aluminium
Screen-printed polycarbonate, aluminium
Sérigraphie de polycarbonate, aluminium

PIATELLO

Design Enzo Catellani 1988
Catellani & Smith
100 Watt
ø 27 cm – 35 cm
Aluminium, Stahl, Porzellan
Aluminum, steel, porcelain
Aluminium, métal, porcelaine

MAXI ELLE 64

Design Tommaso Cimini 1987
Lumina
300 Watt
H 11 cm, ø 47 cm
Lackiertes Metall
Painted metal
Métal peint

URSA MINOR / URSA MAJOR

Design Vico Magistretti 1993
Nemo S.r.l.
50 Watt / 1000 Watt
H max. 225 cm, ø 15 cm / 27 cm
Aluminium, Glas
Aluminum, glass
Aluminium, verre

NYHAVN

Design Alfred Homann und Ole V. Kjær 1982
Louis Poulsen & Co. GmbH
75 Watt
H 21,5 cm, ø 31 cm,
Metall oder Kupfer
Metal or copper
Métal ou cuivre

ILÓ-ILÚ

Design Ingo Maurer und Team 1986
Ingo Maurer GmbH
50 Watt
L 140 cm – 190 cm
Metall, Glas, Kunststoff
Metal, glass, plastic
Métal, verre, matière synthétique

Niedervolt-Mobile mit Umlenkspiegel

Low-voltage mobile with mirrors
to redirect light

Lampe-mobile basse tension
avec miroir déflecteur

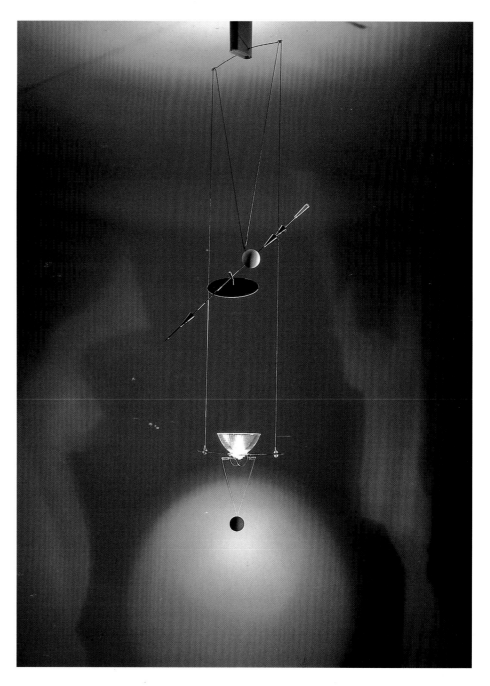

UNO

Design Erwin Egli, Diego Bally
System Diego Bally 1990
Belux
50 Watt
Verchromtes Metall, Glas
Chromium-plated metal, glass
Métal chromé, verre

Höhenverstellbare Niedervoltleuchte
mit Gegengewicht in Senkbleiform

low-voltage lamp with plumb-line
counterweight, height adjustable

Lampe basse tension réglable en
hauteur avec contrepoids en forme
de fil à plomb

 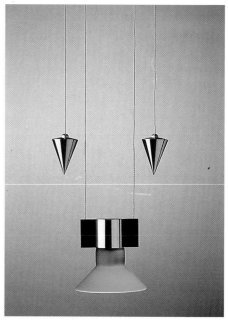

AGGREGATO SOSPENSIONE

Design Enzo Mari 1976
Artemide
100 Watt
H 135 cm – 335 cm
Metall, metal, métal

HMB 25 / 500 Z NI

Design Marianne Brandt, Hans Przyrembel 1925
Tecnolumen
100 Watt
H max. 250 cm, ø 50 cm
Aluminium, aluminum

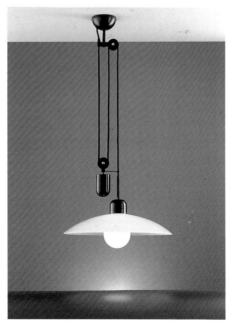

BALA METALICA

Design Equipo Metalarte 1986
Metalarte S. A.
100 Watt
H 130 cm – 325 cm, ø 510 mm
Metall, lackiert
Painted metal
Métal peint

BALA ACRYLIC

Design Equipo Metalarte 1986
Metalarte S. A.
100 Watt
H 130 cm – 325 cm, ø 510 mm
Metall, lackiert, Acrylglas
Painted metal, acrylic glass
Métal peint, verre acrylique

TRANS-IT

Design Sergi Devesa 1988
Metalarte S. A.
50 Watt
H 78 cm - 146 cm
Metall, metal, métal

GEMINI

Design Maurizio Ferrari 1990
Solzi Luce S.r.l.
50 Watt
Alu-Druckguß, Polycarbonat
Die-cast aluminum, polycarbonate
Aluminium coulé sous pression,
polycarbonate

Miniaturisierte Punktstrahler
mit diversen Streuscheiben

Miniature accent spotlight with
diverse kinds of diffuser glass

Spots en miniature avec plusieurs
verres diffusants

DELPHI D

Design Andrea Castelli, Fabio Rezzonico 1988
Segno S.r.l.
75 Watt
L 200 cm
Metall, Glas
Metal, glass
Métal, verre

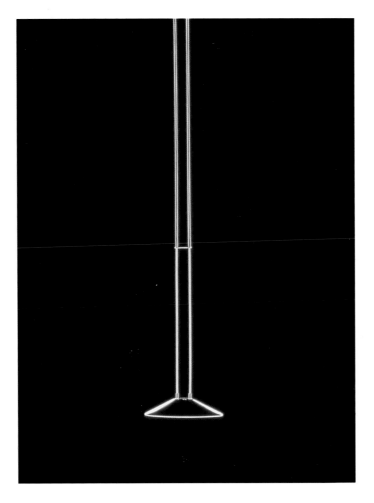

REGINA

Design Jorge Pensi 1988
B. lux
150 Watt
H 170 cm, B 25 cm
Aluminium poliert, Stahl
Polished aluminium, stainless steel
Aluminium brossé, acier

OLYMPIA

Design Jorge Pensi 1988
B.lux
2 x 150 Watt, RS7
H 90 cm –170 cm, B 47 cm
Aluminium, aluminum

Spanischer »Bollidismo« :
Doppelstrahler aus Aluguß

Spanish »Bollidismo«: double
accent light of cast aluminum

«Bollidismo» espagnol: projecteur
double en fonte d'aluminium

LUCIA 3

Design Cini Boeri 1988
Venini S.p.a.
50 Watt
H 160 cm, ø 21 cm
Opalglas, lackierter oder verchromter Stahl
Opal glass, painted or chromium-plated steel
Verre opalescent peint ou acier chromé

Blütenkelche in Muranoglas

Calyxes of Murano glass

Corolles de fleurs en verre de Murano

ALESIA

Design Carlo Forcolini 1982
Artemide
55 Watt, 12 Volt, PK 22 s
H 82 cm – 210 cm, B 32 cm
Metall, metal, métal

Deckenrosette mit Transformator,
Leuchtenschirm an starrem Metallrohr

Ceiling rosette containing transformer,
lampshade on a stiff, metal tube

Plafonnier en rosette avec transformateur,
abat-jour fixé sur tube de métal rigide

CRISOL

Design Perry A. King, Santiago Miranda,
Gianluigi Arnaldi 1981
Flos S.p.a.; koll. Arteluce
55 Watt
H 8,3 cm, B 24,3 cm, D 9,3

Preßglasleuchte mit diffuser
und direkter Abstrahlung

Lamp, pressed glass, for diffuse
as well as direct lighting

Lampe en verre moulé à éclairage
diffus et direct

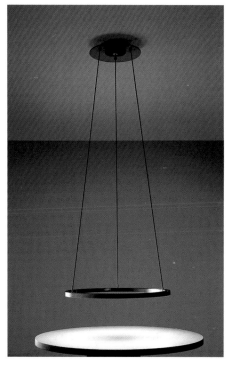

ANTARES

Design Hatto Grosse 1989
Anta Leuchten GmbH
50 Watt, GX 5,3
H 150 cm, ø 12 cm
Aluminium, aluminum

ANELLO

Design Rolf Heide 1988
Anta Leuchten GmbH
9 x 20 Watt, 6 x 20 Watt
H 200 cm, ø 80 cm / 60 cm
Messing, brass, laiton

Neun- oder sechsflammige minimalistische Lichtkrone, extern dimmbar

Minimalist circle of light, nine or six bulbs, externally dimmable

Lustre minimaliste à neuf ou six branches, intensité lumineuse réglable de l'extérieur

TAI-LANG

Design Tobias Grau 1991
Tobias Grau KG GmbH & Co.
5 x 20 Watt, 12 Volt, G 6,35
H 70 cm, B 14 cm
Aluminium, Bronze
Aluminum, bronze
Aluminium, bronze

Spindelförmige Leuchte mit Gegengewicht
Spindle-shaped lamp with counter-weight
Lampe en forme de fuseau avec contrepoids

TAI

Design Tobias Grau 1989
Tobias Grau KG GmbH & Co.
1 x 50 Watt, 12 Volt, G 6,35
ø 18 cm
Aluminium, Bronze
Aluminum, bronze
Aluminium, bronze

Schlichter Reflektor aus kostbarem Material,
höhenverstellbar mit Gegengewicht

Simple reflector made of precious material
with counterweight, height adjustable

Réflecteur simple en matériel précieux,
réglable en hauteur avec contrepoids

AS 41 Z

Design Franco Albini, Franca Helg,
Antonio Piva 1969
Sirrah
150 Watt, E 27
H 100 cm – 34 cm, ø 45 cm
Verchromtes oder vergoldetes Metall
Chromium-plated or gold-plated metal
Métal chromé ou doré

Zweiteiliger Gelenkarm ,
Abstrahlwinkel des Reflektors verstellbar

Two-part jointed arm,
angle of reflector adjustable

Bras articulé en deux parties,
angle d'éclairage du réflecteur réglable

SILVER BULLET

Design Johan Lemaitre 1992
Waco
50 Watt, TAL 50
H max. 22,5 cm
Gebürstetes Aluminium
Brushed aluminium
Aluminium brossé

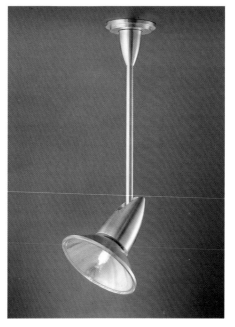 

D 7

Design Sandro Colbertaldo,
Paolo Rizzatto 1980
Luceplan
300 Watt, 220 Volt, GY 9,5
H 208 cm / 178 cm
Aluminium-Preßguß
Die-cast aluminium
Aluminium coulé sous pression

Drehbares stählernes Gelenk mit
pneumatischem Gasdruckdämpfer

Revolving steel joint with pneumatic
gas pressure damper

Articulation d'acier pivotante avec
amortisseur pneumatique à gaz

SOSIA

Design Ufficio Technico Castaldi 1985
Castaldi
150 Watt
H 66,5 cm, ø 42 cm
Alu-Druckguß, Glas, Nylon-Fiberglas
Die-cast aluminium, glass, nylon fibre-glass
Aluminium coulé sous pression, verre,
stratifié à fibre de verre en nylon

Industrieleuchte für High-Tech-Interieurs

Industrial light for high-tech interiors

Lampe industrielle pour intérieurs high-tech

SPUN

Design Paul Newman 1991
Aero Wholesale Ltd.
150 Watt
H 19 cm, ø 29 cm / H 29 , ø 22 cm
H 26,5 cm, ø 11,5 cm / H 33 cm, ø 41,5 cm
Aluminium, aluminum

EMAIL-AMATUR

Louis Poulsen & Co. GmbH
100 / 200 Watt AGL, 13 Watt TD-C
H 22 cm, ø 35 cm, H 31 cm, ø 45 cm

Archetypische Arbeitsleuchte aus
emailliertem Stahlblech

Archetypal work-lamp made of enamelled sheet steel

Lampe de bureau archétypique en tôle émaillée

WAND- UND DECKENLEUCHTEN

WALL AND CEILING LIGHTS

APPLIQUES ET PLAFONNIERS

Die ersten Wandleuchten waren vermutlich brennende Fackeln in Wandhalterungen. Im Barock wurden in größeren Räumen, in denen Kronleuchter brannten, die Wände mit Vergoldungen und Spiegeln verziert, die das zentrale Licht von der Decke wie indirekte Wandleuchten reflektierten und verstärkten. Kandelaber und Armleuchter streckten später ihre Halterungen weit in den Raum hinein. Wandleuchten strahlen immer einen Hauch von Festlichkeit und Gediegenheit aus. Heute werden sie direkt an die Mauer montiert und bestehen meist nur aus einem Schirm ohne sichtbare Halterung. »Wall-Washer« lenken das Licht vertikal an der Wand entlang und erzeugen großflächige, vorhangartige Lichtfelder, in denen zuweilen das Mauerrelief wirkungsvoll hervortritt. Meist sind Wand- und Deckenleuchten nur Adaptionen von Hänge- oder Stehleuchten. Aufgeschnittene Kugeln oder Halbschalen geben teils gerichtetes, teils diffuses Licht. Weil Wand- und Deckenleuchten meist in Zweier- oder Dreiergruppen angebracht werden und selten punktgenau einzelne Bereiche erhellen, strahlen sie eine ähnliche Verschwendungslust aus wie frühere Kronleuchter. Den wahren Zauber von Wandleuchten zeigen ihre schönsten Ableger: die hinterleuchteten oder mit Birnen umkränzten Spiegel in Künstlergarderoben. Weit vorkragende Wandleuchten dagegen, die nichts anderes als stationär angebrachte Tisch- oder Stehleuchten sind, erweisen sich oft als sperrig und unpraktisch.

The first wall lights were probably burning torches mounted on walls. In the baroque era larger rooms, which were illuminated by chandeliers, had walls decorated with gold and mirrors. They reflected and intensified the central light like indirect wall lights. The mounts of candelabras and chandeliers later stretched well into the room. Wall lights always have an air of ceremony and solidity about them. Nowadays they are fixed directly to the wall and usually consist of a shade and a concealed mount. »Wall washers« direct the light vertically across the wall and produce broad, curtain-like areas of light in which the texture of the wall sometimes stands out effectively.
Usually wall and ceiling lights are simply adaptations of suspended or standard lamps. Cut-open spheres and hemispheres can give off focussed light or diffuse light. Because wall and ceiling lights usually appear in twos or threes and rarely illuminate an exact point, they have a similar decadent wastefulness about them to the chandelier. The most beautiful variations of wall lights best show their true magic: they are the back-lit or circum-lit mirrors in the dressing-rooms of artists. However, protruding wall lights that are nothing but desk or standard lamps that have been fixed to the wall often prove unwieldy and impractical.

Les premières appliques étaient probablement des flambeaux fixés aux murs. A l'époque baroque, les murs des grandes salles étaient ornés de dorures et de miroirs qui reflétaient et renforçaient la lumière du lustre situé au centre du plafond. Les candélabres et les chandeliers n'intervinrent que plus tard. Les appliques évoquent toujours un peu la fête et un solide confort bourgeois. Aujourd'hui elles sont montées directement sur le mur et on ne voit d'elles qu'un écran sans support visible. Les «wall-washers» dirigent la lumière le long du mur dans le sens vertical et font naître de vastes champs lumineux, des rideaux de lumière, qui font ressortir les reliefs de la paroi.
Les appliques et plafonniers ne sont le plus souvent que des adaptations de lampes à suspension et de lampadaires. Des boules entaillées ou des hémisphères engendrent une lumière diffuse ou dirigée. Comme les appliques et les plafonniers sont le plus souvent placés par groupes de deux ou trois et qu'ils n'éclairent que rarement des zones précises, ils procèdent au fond du même esprit dissipateur que les lustres d'autrefois. La magie initiale des appliques émane encore des miroirs entourés de lampes ou éclairés de derrière que l'on trouve dans les loges des artistes. Par contre les appliques proéminentes, qui ne sont rien d'autres que des lampes de bureau ou des lampadaires immobilisés, s'avèrent le plus souvent encombrantes et peu pratiques.

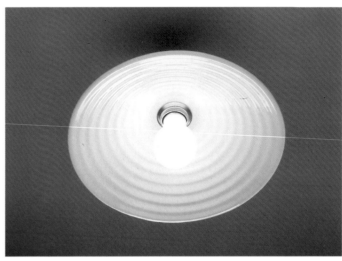

LF-2064

Design Yamada Shomei
Yamada Shomei Lighting Co.
40 Watt
D 16,5 cm, ø 62 cm
Holz, Kunststoff
Wood, plastic
Bois, plastique

BRERA

Design Achille Castiglioni 1992
Flos S.p.a.
100 Watt / 23 Watt
H 26 cm, B 14 cm
Glas, Kunststoff
Glass, plastic
Verre, plastique

LF-8125

Design Yamada Shomei
Yamada Shomei Lighting Co.
70 Watt
H 12 cm, ø 50 cm
Metall, Kunststoff
Metal, plastic
Métal, plastique

EDISON 35

Design Valerio Sacchetti 1989
Sirrah
100 Watt
H 11,5 cm, ø 31 cm
Emailkeramik
Enamel ceramic
Céramique émaillée

METROPOLI

Design Alberto Meda, Paolo Rizzatto 1992
Luceplan
300 W
ø 17 cm / 27 cm / 38 cm / 56 cm
Diffusor aus Glas oder Polycarbonat
in Scharnierrahmen
Glass or polycarbonate diffuser
in hinge-frame
Diffuseur en verre ou polycarbonate
dans un cadre-charnière

LUCI FAIR

Design Phillippe Starck 1989
Flos S.p.a.
150 Watt
H 30 cm, B 14 cm / 24 cm
Porzellan, Messing, Metall
Porcelain, brass, metal
Porcelaine, laiton, métal

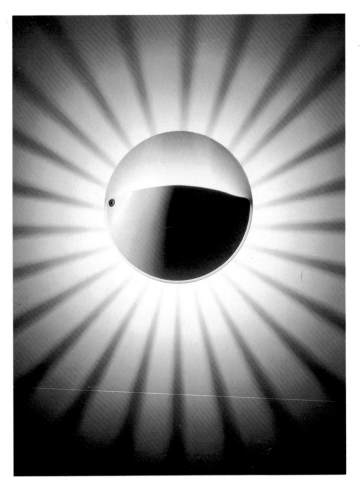

GIOVI

Design Achille Castiglioni 1982
Flos S.p.a.
1 x 150 Watt
D 16 cm, ø 28 cm
Lackiertes Metall
Painted metal
Métal peint

Wall-Washer mit Sunrise-Schattenspiel
Wallwasher with sunrise shadow play
Diffuseur de lumière mural avec
«lever du soleil» et jeu d'ombres

QUARTO

Design Tobias Scarpa 1973
Flos S.p.a.
75 Watt
H 18,3 cm, B 40 cm, D 21 cm
Metall, Messing
Metal, brass
Métal, laiton

Klassischer Wall-Washer, halbmondförmig
Classic wallwasher, half-moon shaped
Diffuseur demi-lune de lumière classique

WAD 37 CSW

Design 1937
Tecnolumen
100 Watt, 220 Volt, E 27 / 500 Watt, 220 Volt, R 7s
H 9 cm, L 48 cm
Chrom und schwarz lackiertes Holz
Chromium and black painted wood
Chrome et bois peint en noir

Pseudosakrale Opferschalenform im
Monumentalstil der dreißiger Jahre
Dish shaped as pseudosacred sacrifice dish
in the monumental style of the 'Thirties
Lampe en forme de coupe sacrificielle dans
le style monumental des années trente

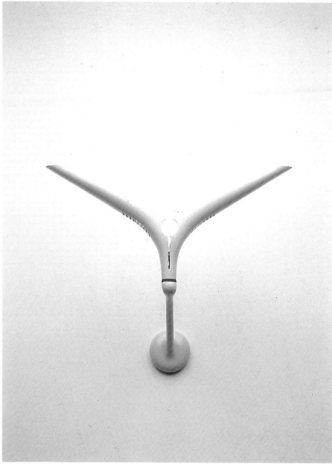

ORIO

Design Sergio Mazza 1973
quattrifolio S.p.a.
3 x 60 Watt
H 50 cm
Kunststoff, Metall
Plastic, metal
Matière synthétique, métal

TUKANA PARETE

Design Carlo Forcolini 1993
Nemo S.r.l.
300 Watt
H 33,5 cm, L 27 cm, B 45 cm,
Glas, Aluminium-Druckguß
Glass, die-cast aluminium
Verre, aluminium coulé sous pression

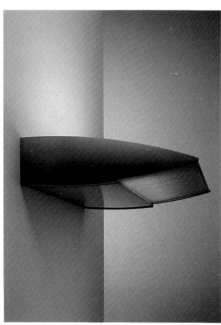

B 2036 R

Design Grenwemon 1992
Yamagiwa Corporation
40 Watt
H 37 cm, B 26 cm, D 16,5 cm
Chinaware, Papier
Fine bone china, paper
Porcelaine de Chine, papier

ECONOMY

Design Jürgen Medebach 1992
Belux
2 x TC-I 36 Watt
Metall, metal, métal

Superflache, indirekt strahlende Bürowandleuchte,
wahlweise mit sensorgesteuerter Mehrstufenschaltung

Superflat wall-light for office use, lights indirectly,
optional sensor-controlled variable lighting

Applique de bureau ultraplate à éclairage
indirect, au choix gradateur commandé par palpeur

LAZZURRO

Design Frans van Niewenborg, Wegmann 1992
Nieuwenborg / Wegmann
58 / 36 Watt
H 150 cm / 120 cm
Kunststoff
Plastic
Matière synthétique

Futuristischer Lichtpfeil in gespanntem Bogen

Futurist »arrow« of light in drawn bow

Flèche de lumière futuriste dans un arc tendu

LI LI

Design G. Arnaldi, L. Gaetani 1991
Status srl
50 / 100 W max, 12 Volt
H 75 cm, L 8 cm, D 7 cm
Aluminium, Technopolymer
Aluminum, technopolymer
Aluminium, technopolymère

Wandleuchte mit nach Bedarf
orientierbarem Leuchtenpendel

Wall-light with adjustable light pendant

Applique murale avec lampes sur
balancier orientable

ZERO ONE

Design Ingo Maurer 1990
Ingo Maurer GmbH
75 Watt,
L 28 cm, ø 17 cm
Weißes Corian
White Corian
Corian blanc

Variation von Tatlins Eck-Kontra-Relief:
Antennenstab mit Reflektorscheibe

Variation on Tatlin's corner-counter-relief:
aerial with a reflector

Variation du Eck-Kontra-Relief de Tatlin:
antenne et disque réflecteur

1292 ZHP

Design Elio Martinelli 1992
Martinelli Luce S.p.a.
150 Watt
H 40 cm
Metall, metal, métal

WARRIOR

Design Emanuelle Ricci 1991
Sidecar
150 Watt
H 18 cm, L 20 cm, B 22 cm
Lackierter Kunststoff, verchromtes
Metall, metallisiertes Glas
Painted plastic, chromium-plated
metal, metal-plated glass
Matière synthétique peinte, métal
chromé, verre métallisé

WAL 17D

Design Daí Design 1992
Belux
300 Watt
H 175 cm
Metall, metal, métal

In Höhe der Fußleiste montierbare Wandleuchte mit drehbarem Reflektorschirm

Wall-light with adjustable reflector shade,
can be affixed at skirting-board level

Applique murale montable à hauteur
des plinthes, réflecteur pivotant

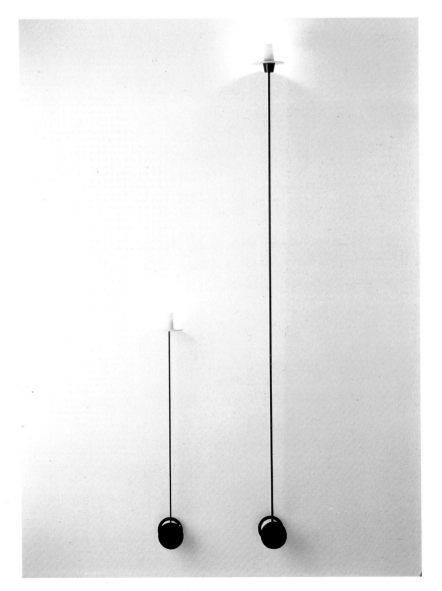

DEA

Design De Pas, D´Urbino, Lomazzi 1986
Noto / Zeus S.r.l.
150 Watt
H 83 cm, B 11 cm, D 9 cm
Aluminiumgestell, Porzellanschirm
Aluminum frame, porcelain shade
Support en aluminium,
abat-jour en porcelaine

In Höhe der Fußleiste
montierbare Wandleuchte

Wall-light which can be affixed
at skirting-board level

Applique murale montable
à hauteur des plinthes

DILEM PARETE

Design Umberto Riva 1992
Fontana Arte
60 Watt
H 38 cm, B 25 cm, D 20 cm

LIZAR

Design Jean Francois Crochet
Sergio Terzani & C.s.n.c.
50 Watt
H 19 cm, ø 10 cm
Eisen, iron, fer

Mischung aus Rokoko und Arte povera:
historisierender doppelarmiger Leuchter

Mixture of rococo and arte povera styles:
historicist double-armed light

Mélange de Rococo et d'Arte povera:
lampadaire à deux branches

PORTAFRUTTA

Design Dennis Santachiara 1989
Domodinamica S.r.l.
H 32 cm, B 10 cm, D 35 cm
Aluminium, aluminum

Ein poetischer Entwurf: beleuchtete Obstschale in
Wandhalterung in der Tradition des Radical Design

Wall-light shaped like an illuminated fruit bowl
mounted on a wall, a poetic light in the
tradition of Radical Design

Poésie pure: coupe à fruits éclairée fixée à un
support mural dans la tradition du Radical design

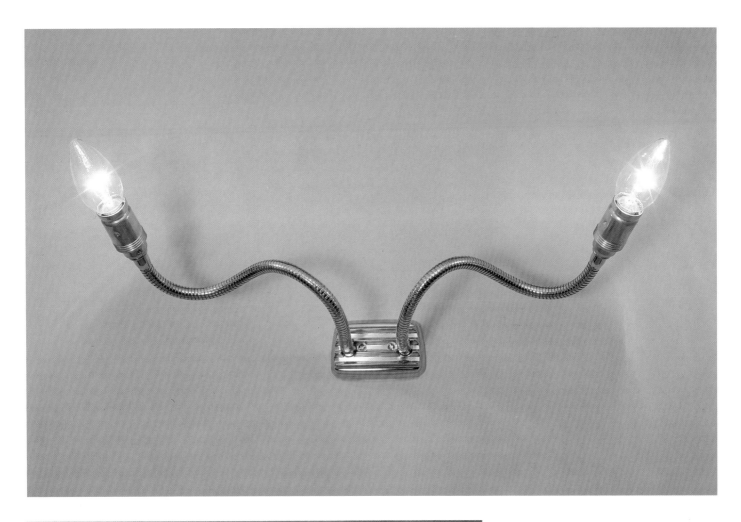

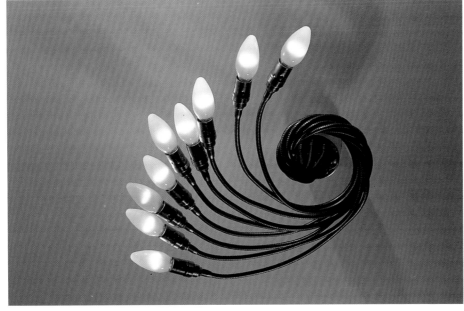

SUZUKI

Design Stiletto Studios 1988
Stiletto Studios
25 Watt
B 8,5 cm, L 35 cm, D 5 cm
Verchromter Schwanenhals, polierter
Aluminiumsockel, Metallfassungen
Chromium-plated swan's neck, polished
aluminum mount, metal holders
Col de cygne chromé, socle d'aluminium
poli, supports en métal

Berliner Ready-made-Design aus
Mikrofonhalterung

Ready-made design from Berlin
with microphone stand

Ready-Made berlinois à partir
d'un support de micro

TURCIÙ PARETE

Design Enzo Catellani 1992
Catellani & Smith
8 x 60 Watt, E 14, 220 Volt
H 50 cm, L 25 cm
Metall, metal, métal

Bündel dekorativer »Schwanenhälse«, goldfarben
Bundle of decorative »swans' necks«, gold in colour
Faisceau de cols de cygnes dorés

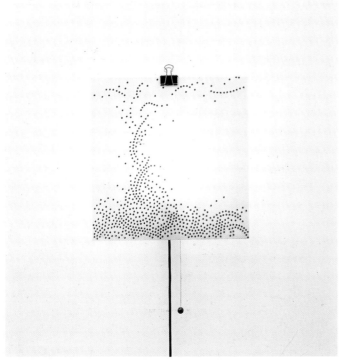

Fumikazu Masuda

Siggi Fischer

Filipe Alarcaó

Hironen

Nic Bewick

Stiletto

COPYLIGHT EDITION KOPIE

**Design Meta Moderne,
Dietz Design Management 1993
Thomas Schulte, Design Box
40 Watt
H 30 cm, B 30 cm, D 12 cm
Zinkblech, Acrylglas
Sheet-zinc, acrylic glass
Tôle de zinc, verre acrylique**

Design aus dem Fotokopierer: Lampenschirme von internationalen Designern, die auf einen schlichten Wechselrahmen gespannt werden. Erlesenes Design aus der Vervielfältigungsmaschine, das den Unterschied zwischen Original und Kopie einebnet.

Design from the photocopier: lampshades by international designers are stretched onto a simple clip-on frame. Exquisite design from the photocopier eliminates the disparity between original and copy.

Design né de la photocopieuse: des abat-jour de concepteurs internationaux tendus sur un cadre tout simple. Un design de haute qualité issu de la photocopieuse, et qui atténue la différence entre l'original et la copie

Pedro Silva Dias

Guen Bertheau Suzuki

Guen Bertheau Suzuki

Gruppe X 99

Luigi Serafini

Alberto Lievore & Asociados

Formfürsorge

Juli Capella & Quim Larrea

Rafael Jiménez & Claudia Casagrande

Timothy Stebbing

Timothy Stebbing

Catarina Ferreira

Hideo Mori

Michele de Lucchi

Alessandro Mendini

James Irvine

Kenji Oki & Hisako Watanabe

Konstantin Grcic

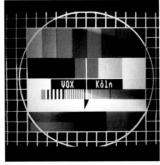

Ben Bleibe

Aldo Cibic

STEHLEUCHTEN   STANDARD LAMPS   LAMPADAIRES

Eine frühe Variante von Stehleuchten gab es an europäischen Fürstenhöfen. Wenn die Herrschaften zu Bett gingen, mußte ihnen nicht nur ein Diener den Weg ausleuchten, sondern oft die ganze Nacht neben dem Bett stehen, die Öllampe halten und aufpassen, daß sie nicht erlosch. Heute sind Stehlampen die vielseitigsten und meistverwendeten Lichtquellen. Sie spiegeln deutlich den Trend zum »Schneller-Wohnen«. Nach den alten Modellen mit schweren Standbeinen und ausladenden Pilz-Schirmen erlaubt heute die Halogentechnik verschwindend kleine Lampenköpfe. Im Vergleich dazu erscheinen die Lampenständer, selbst bei reduziertester Ausführung, oft unproportioniert groß. Man betrachte einmal Stehleuchten aus umgekehrter Richtung, als sei der Raum auf den Kopf gestellt. Dann wird klar, wie monströs manche Substruktionen und wie nichtig die Lichtquellen sind. Es gibt Modelle, die grazil wie Flamingos auf einem Bein stehen, und andere, die ehrfurchtgebietend wie sakrale Stelen wirken. Gemeinsam ist den meisten neueren Entwürfen, daß sie flutlichtartig die Decken anstrahlen, wie es schon einmal während der Art Déco-Ära beliebt gewesen war. Die punktgenauen, höhenverstellbaren Modelle dagegen werden heute seltener eingesetzt.

An early variation of the standard lamp could be found in royal palaces across Europe. When the lords and ladies retired, their servant not only lit the way for them, but often had to stand next to the bed all night holding the oil lamp and making sure it did not burn out. Nowadays standard lamps are the most versatile and commonly used sources of light. They clearly reflect the trend toward »faster living«. After the old models with heavy legs and projecting mushroom-shaped lampshades, modern halogen technology mekes quite minute lampheads. In comparison the lampstands often appear disproportionately large, even in their most reduced form. If one were to look at standard lamps the other way up, as though the room were upside down, it would become clear how monstrous some substructures are and how trifling the actual lamps are. Some lamps stand on one leg like a graceful flamingo, while others that look like sacred steles are quite awe-inspiring. Newer designs generally illuminate the ceiling like floodlights, much in the Art Déco fashion. Exactly focussed lights whose height can be adjusted are used more rarely nowadays.

Remontons le cours de l'Histoire pour assister au Coucher du Roi: le valet devait non seulement le guider en l'éclairant mais aussi rester toute la nuit debout à côté du lit du souverain, lampadaire avant l'heure, la lampe à huile à la main et veillant à ce qu'elle ne s'éteigne pas. Les lampadaires sont devenus les sources de lumière les plus complexes et les plus utilisées. Ils reflètent clairement la tendance moderne au «nomadisme». Les anciens modèles avaient des pieds massifs et de vastes abat-jour en chapeau de champignon, les lampadaires halogènes, quant à eux, ont des lampes extrêmement petites et des supports exagérément volumineux. Si on regarde un lampadaire la tête en bas, on se rend compte de la monstruosité de certains supports et on constate que les sources de lumière sont pratiquement inexistantes, c'est comme si la pièce était, elle aussi, retournée. Certains modèles ont la grâce de flamants roses en équilibre sur une jambe, d'autres, semblables à des stèles, inspirent la vénération. Presque tous les nouveaux modèles éclairent les plafonds à la manière de projecteurs d'ambiance, comme on l'appréciait déjà au temps de l'Art déco. Par contre on utilise plus rarement aujourd'hui les lampadaires réglables en hauteur et dont la lumière se concentre sur un point fixe.

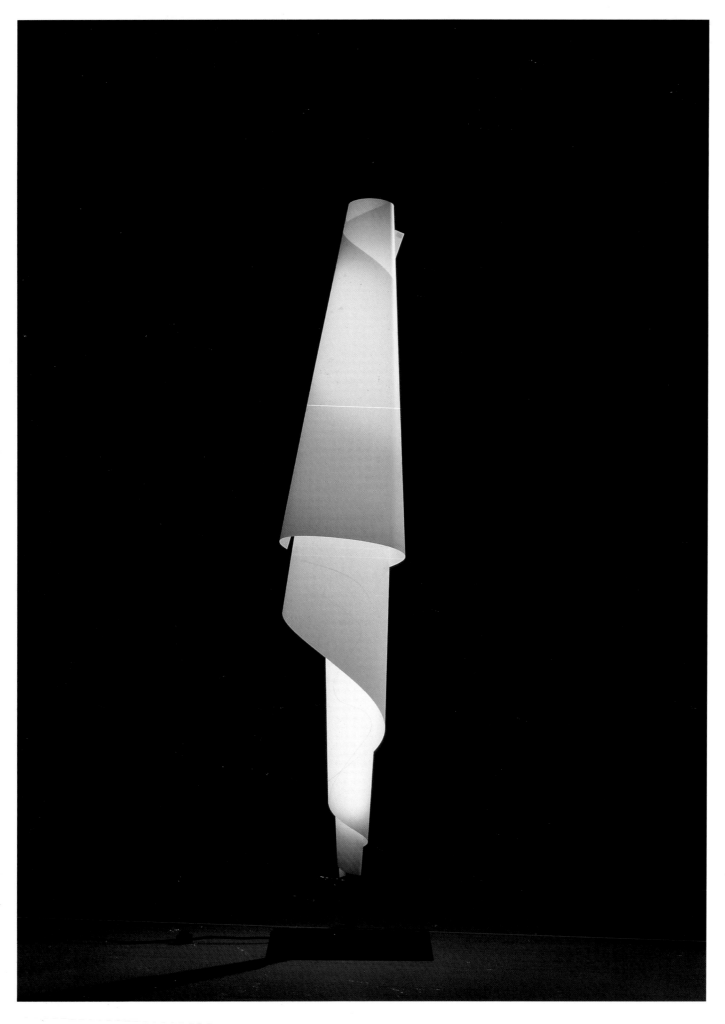

TMM

Design Miquel Milá 1961
Santa & Cole
100 Watt
H 165 cm, B 50 cm
Holz, Metall, Papier
Wood, metal, paper
Bois, métal, papier

Volkskunst: Weiterentwicklungen der
traditionellen katalanischen Stehleuchte

Folk art: further development of a
traditional Catalan standard lamp

Art populaire: perfectionnement du
lampadaire catalan traditionnel

NORDICA

Design Equipo Santa & Cole 1987
Santa & Cole
60 Watt
H 140 cm, B 30 cm
Holz, Metall, Papier
Wood, metal, paper
Bois, métal, papier

ALTA COSTURA

Design Josep Aregall 1992
Metalarte S. A.
120 Watt + 60 Watt
H 220 cm / 260 cm, B 50 cm

Spanische Materialästhetik: Wie eine herabfallende
Stoffbahn scheint »alta costura« zu schweben

Spanish aesthetics of material: »alta costura«
seems to float like a falling length of cloth

Esthétisme espagnol: Alta Costura semble planer
comme une draperie tombant à terre

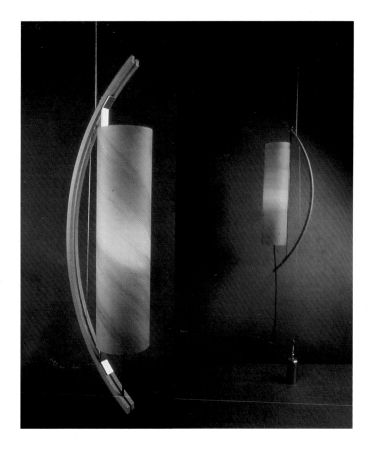

ARCO

Design Mariona Raventós, Jordi Miralbell 1983
Santa & Cole
60 Watt
H 90 cm
Holz, Papier, Metall
Wood, metal, paper
Bois, papier, métal

CALIDA

Design Pete Sans 1988
DLC S. A., »Taller Uno«
60 Watt
H 161 cm, ø 14 cm
Verchromtes Metall, Schirm: Pergament
Chromium-plated metal, parchment shade
Métal chromé, abat-jour en parchemin

Edle Sparsamkeit: spanische Kombination
von Naturmaterial und warmen Tönen

Fine frugality: Spanish combination of
natural materials and warm colours

Economie mais noblesse des matériaux naturels: combinaison espagnole aux tons chauds

TEA

Design C. Lalastra, J. Rada
B. Lux
11 Watt
H 120 cm / 150 cm, ø 22 cm
Verchromtes oder vermessingtes
Metall, Alabaster, Holz
Chromium-plated or brass-plated
metal, alabaster, wood
Métal chromé ou laitonné, albâtre, bois

CLARIS

Design Porqueras 1992
Mobles 114
60 Watt
H 16 cm / 25 cm
Kunststoff, Opalglas
Plastic, glass
Matériel synthétique, verre opalescent

LA BELLA DURMIENTE
Design Gabriel Ordeig 1986
Santa & Cole
58 Watt
H 180 cm, B 25 cm, D 25 cm
Kunststoff, Metall
Plastic, wood
Matière synthétique, métal

Lichttotem aus bedrucktem Pergament

Totem of light made of printed parchment.

«Totem» de lumière en parchemin imprimé

TUBE LIGHT
Design Eileen Gray 1927
ClassiCon GmbH
H 102 cm
Verchromtes Stahlgestell
Chromium-plated steel frame
Support d'acier chromé

Damals radikal modernes Röhrendesign,
heute ein stilvoller Klassiker

A radically modern tube design at the time,
nowadays this has become a stylish classic

A l'époque un design tubulaire radicalement
moderne; aujourd'hui un classique élégant

FORTUNY

Design Marano Fortuny, Mariano Madrazo 1907
Pallucco Italia S.a.s.
500 W
H max. 240 cm, B 93,5 cm, D 82 cm
Stahl, Schirm: Baumwolle
Steel, cotton shade
Acier, abat-jour en coton

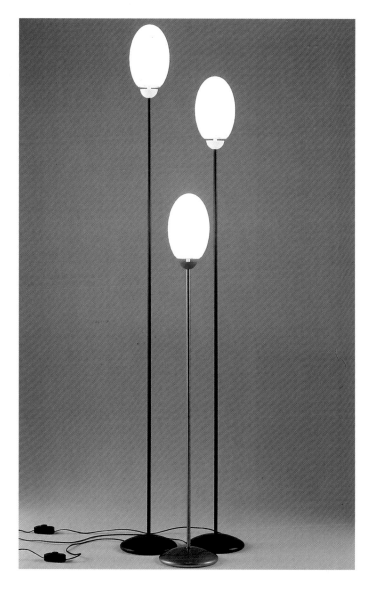

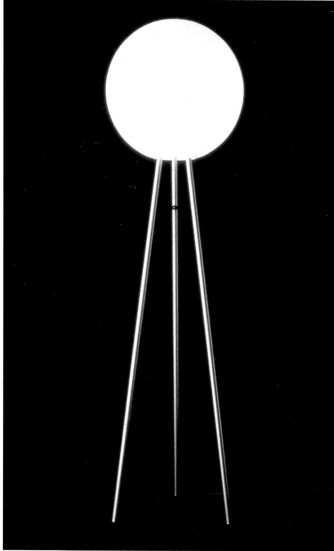

BRERA

Design Achille Castiglioni 1992
Flos S.p.a.
100 Watt
H 134 / 178 / 197 cm
Glas, Kunststoff, Metall
Glass, plastic, metal
Verre, plastique, métal

Neues vom Altmeister:
eine minimalistische Zimmerlaterne

New design from an old master:
a minimalist lantern for the interior

Une nouveauté de la main du vieux
maître: lanterne d'intérieur minimaliste

PRIMA SIGNORA

Design Daniela Puppa 1992
Fontana Arte
250 Watt, 220 Volt, E 27
H 170 cm, ø 50 cm
Glas, Metall
Glass, metal
Verre, métal

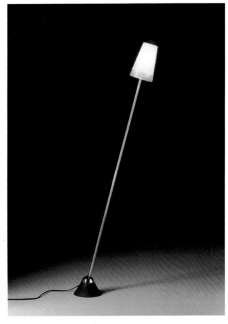

MAGNITA

Design Pete Sans 1989
Metalarte
40 Watt
H 106 cm, ø 15 cm
Gummifuß, Metall,
Aluminium, Pergament
Rubber base, metal,
aluminum, parchment
Pied en caoutchouc, métal,
aluminium, parchemin

SINCLINA

Design Estudi Blanc 1990
Metalarte
100 Watt
H 150 cm, ø 35 cm
Metall, Opalglas
Metal, opal glass
Métal, verre opalescent

CORONA

Design Vincenzo Porcelli 1987
Luxo Italiana S.p.a.
75 Watt
H 132 cm, ø 40 cm

Stilisierte Sonnenscheibe aus Reispapier
Stylized sun disc made of rice-paper
Soleil stylisé en papier de riz

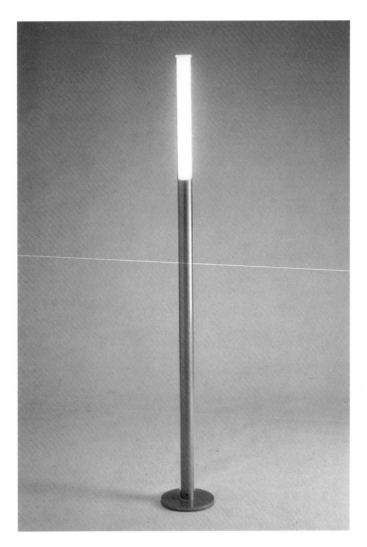

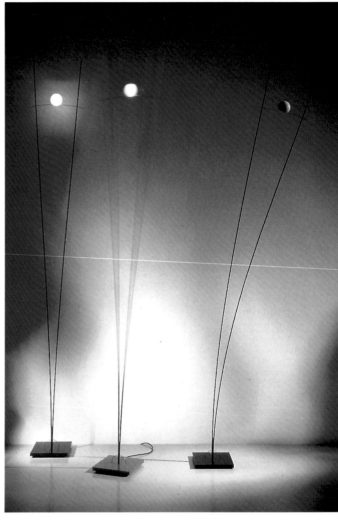

TOBOSO

Design Valerio Sacchetti 1992
Sirrah
55 Watt
H 190 cm, ø 24 cm
Gestell und Sockel aus lackiertem Metall, Schirm
aus Opalmethacrylat, Reflektor aus Aluminium
Frame and mount painted metal, opal
methacrylate shade, aluminum reflector
Support et socle en métal peint, abat-jour en
méthacrylate opalin, réflecteur en aluminium

Stilisierung eines Kerzenhalters

Stylized version of a candelabra

Chandelier stylisé

ILIOS

Design Ingo Maurer, Franz Ringelhan 1983
Ingo Maurer GmbH
50 Watt
H 190 cm, B 18, D 18 cm
Metall, Glas
Metal, glass
Métal, verre

Entmaterialisierte Niedervoltstele

Dematerialized low-voltage stele

Lampe basse tension: stèle dématérialisée

SWING

Design Lorenza Sussarello
Guy Brantschen 1990
L´Aquilone
75 Watt
H 75 cm
Metall, Kunststoffgewebe
Metal, Plastic tissue
Métal, matière synthétique

DUO TERRA

Design Luciano Baelstrini, Paola Longhi 1992
Lumina
250 Watt
H max. 168 cm, ø 32 cm
Metall und Polycarbonat
Metal and polycarbonate
Métal et polycarbonate

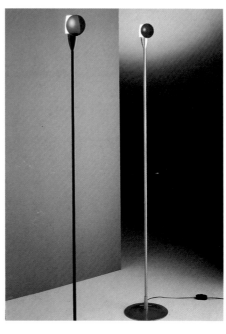

LAMPADA DI MILO

Design Alessandro Mendini 1987
Segno srl.
250 Watt
H 170 cm, ø 34 cm

Farbig lackierter Metallkubus
mit Opalglaskugel

Metal cube painted different colours
with opal glass ball

Cube de métal peint en couleur
avec boule de verre opalin

BLOB

Design Hans von Klier 1992
Bilumen
150 Watt
H 192 cm, ø 10 cm
Metall, sandgestrahltes Glas
Metal, sand-blasted glass
Métal, verre décapé au sable

PAPILLONA

Design Tobia Scarpa 1976
Flos S.p.a.
300 – 500 Watt
H 192 cm, B 26 cm
Glas, Aluminium
Glass, aluminum
Verre, aluminium

Schlanke Halogenstele, die mit prismatischen
Diffusorscheiben des Schirms den seitlichen
Lichtaustritt zusätzlich betont

Slim halogen stele. The shade, consisting of pris-
matically cut pieces of diffuser glass, gives additional
emphasis to the lateral emission of light

Stèle halogène élancée: les disques diffusants
prismatiques de l'abat-jour soulignent la lumière
sortant sur les côtés

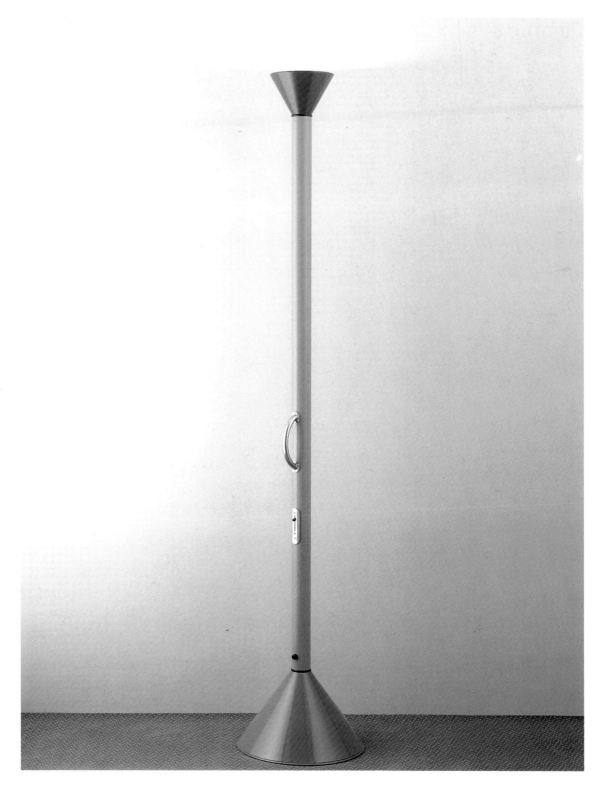

CALLIMACO

Design Ettore Sottsass 1982
Artemide
300 Watt
H 200 cm, ø 40 cm
Metall, metal, métal

Memphis-Klassiker mit überproportional
großem Kegelfuß, dimmbar

Memphis classic with an oversized
conical base, dimmable

Classique du mouvement Memphis, pied-boule
surproportionné, intensité réglable

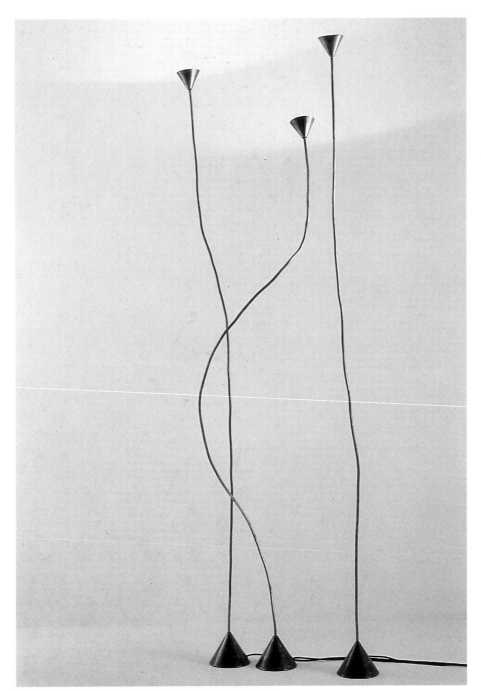

PAPIRO

Design Sergio Calatroni 1988
Pallucco Italia S.a.s.
100 W
H max. 270 cm, ø 16,5 cm
Kupfer
Copper
Cuivre

Biegsam, orientierbar
Flexible and directable
Flexible, orientable

LUMINATOR

Design Pietro Chiesa 1933
Fontana Arte
300 Watt
H 190 cm, ø 22 cm
Messing, lackiert, oder Nickel, gebür-
stet
Painted brass or brushed nickel
Laiton peint ou nickel brossé

Urform der Stehleuchte als
kelchförmiger Deckenstrahler
Archetypal standard lamp,
an over-sized cup-shaped uplight
Forme primitive du lampadaire traité
en tant que plafonnier-corolle

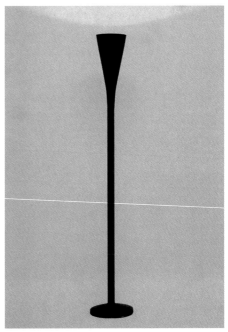

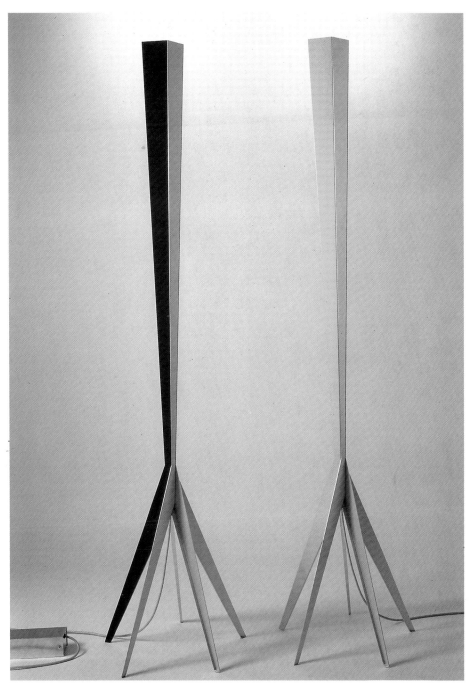

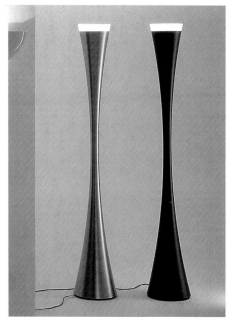

BICONICA

Design Elio Martinelli 1987
Martinelli Luce S.p.a.
250 Watt, HQI 70 Watt
H 175 cm
Kunstharz
Synthetic resin
Résine synthétique

TIBIBI

Design Alberto Meda 1992
Luceplan
250 Watt, 150 Watt
H 185 cm, ø 47 cm
Aluminium, Polyäthylen
Aluminum, polyethylene
Aluminium, polyéthylène

High-Tech, kompakt: aufgefächerte
Metallsegmente, kompakt zusammenlegbar

High-tech, compact: arrangement of
metal segments, compactly foldable

High-tech compact: segments de métal
en éventail et repliables

GABBIANO

Design Guiseppe Linardi 1990
quattrifolio S.p.a.
2 x 150 Watt
H max. 233 cm, B 90 cm
Metall, metal, métal

JILL

Design Perry A. King, Santiago Miranda,
Gianluigi Arnaldi 1978
Flos S.p.a.; koll. Arteluce
300 Watt
H 193 cm
Metall, Glas
Metal, glass
Métal, verre

Stehleuchte mit direktem und diffusem
Licht, Dimmer im Fußteil, Fuß und
Reflektor in farbigem Opalglas

Standard lamp which gives direct as well
as diffuse light. Dimmer in base. Base and
reflector are made of coloured opal glass.

Lampadaire avec lumière directe et diffuse,
intensité lumineuse réglable dans la partie
inférieure, pied et réflecteur dans le verre
opalin coloré

MONTJUIC

Design Santiago Calatrava 1990
Artemide
450 Watt
H 190 cm, B 45 cm
Glas sandgestrahlt, Kunstharz
Sand-blasted glass, synthetic resin
Verre décapé au sable, résine synthétique

Organoide Fackelträgerleuchte des großen
expressionistischen Konstrukteurs aus Spanien

Organic-looking torch-holder. A light designed
by the great Spanish expressionist designer.

Lampe porte-flambeaux d'aspect organique, œuvre
du grand créateur expressionniste espagnol

CLIP

Design G. Arnaldi, L. Gaetani 1991
Status S.r.l.
250 Watt
H 201 cm, B 23 cm, D 6 cm
Aluminium, Kunststoff
Aluminum, plastic
Aluminium, plastique

Raumhohe Klemmleuchte, die zwischen Decke
und Fußboden gespannt wird, Höhe anpaßbar
von 240 bis 320 cm, verstellbarer Lichtaustritt

Ceiling-high clamp-light to be fitted between ceiling
and floor; Height adjustable between 240 and
320 cm; adjustable lighting

Lampe à pince tendue entre le sol et le plafond.
Hauteur adaptable de 240 à 320 cm, sortie
de la lumière réglable

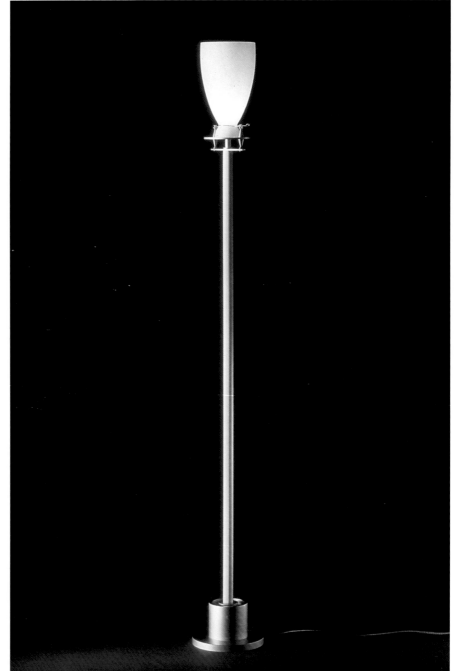

STELE

Design Jürgen Medebach 1991
Belux
400 Watt
H 180 cm
Aluminium, aluminum

Deckenstrahler mit sinnlicher
Oberfläche, Aluminium, metallisiert
Uplight with sensual surface,
metal-plated aluminum
Plafonnier en aluminium métallisé,
la surface évoque la sensualité

FRANCESCHINA

Design Umberto Riva 1989
Fontana Arte
100 Watt
H 175 cm, ø 22 cm
Satiniertes Opalglas, Aluminium oder Messing
Glazed opal glass, aluminum or brass
Verre opalin satiné, aluminium ou laiton

KOHLMARKT

Design Hans Hollein 1985
Baleri
300 Watt
H 235 cm / 275 cm
Aluminium, Messing
Aluminum, brass
Aluminium, laiton

Postmodernes Antikenzitat: Industriestrahler
auf Aluminiumsäule mit Marmordekor,
Messinghalter

Post-modern citation of antiquity: industrial
light mounted on aluminum column with
marble effect, brass holder

Citation antique revue par les post-modernes:
projecteur industriel sur colonne en aluminium avec décor de marbre, fixation en laiton

2235 ZH

Design Elio Martinelli 1992
Martinelli Luce S.p.a.
150 Watt
H 180 cm
Metall
Metal
Métal

Dekoratives High-Tech mit Reflektor
in Kalottenform

Decorative high-tech design with
reflector, shaped as part of hemisphere

High-tech décoratif avec réflecteur
en forme de calotte

FIREBALL

Design Carlo Forcolini 1991
Sidecar
300 Watt
H max. 210 cm, ø 25 cm
Metall, verchromt, lackiert
Chromium-plated metal, painted
Métal chromé et peint

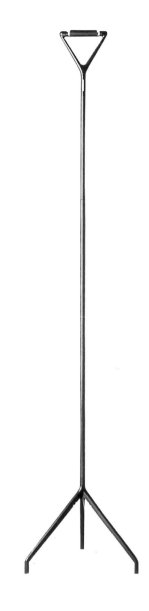

NUNK TERRA

Design Carlo Forcolini 1993
Nemo S.r.l.
75 Watt, 12 Volt
H 122- 165 cm, ø 12 cm
Stahlrohr, Kunststoff
Steel tube, plastic
Tube d'acier, matière synthétique

LOLA

Design Alberto Meda, Paolo Rizzatto 1987
Luceplan
300 Watt
H max. 200 cm, B 18 cm
Kohlefaser, Polyurethan
Carbon fibre, polyurethane
Fibre de carbone, polyuréthane

Funktionelles High-Tech: Teleskopkonstruktion aus ultraleichter Kohlefaser mit Sensordimmer, zusammenlegbarem Fuß

Functional high-tech: telescope construction made of ultra-light carbon fibre with sensor dimmer, collapsible base

High-tech fonctionnel: construction téléscopique en fibre de carbone ultralégère. Intensité lumineuse réglable par palpeur, pied pliable

CICLOCINA TERRA

Design Enzo Catellani 1989
Catellani & Smith
35 Watt, 12 Volt
H 135 cm, L 25 cm
Messing, Eisen, vernickelt
Brass, nickel-plated iron
Laiton, fer

Ready-made aus Fahrradleuchte und »Schwanenhals«

Ready-made from bicycle light and »swan's neck«

Ready-made issu d'une lampe de bicyclette et d'un col de cygne

BIBIP

Design Achille Castiglioni 1976
Flos S.p.a.
H max. 218 cm, ø 23 cm
Stahl, Aluminium, Porzellan
Steel, aluminum, porcelain
Acier, aluminium, porcelaine

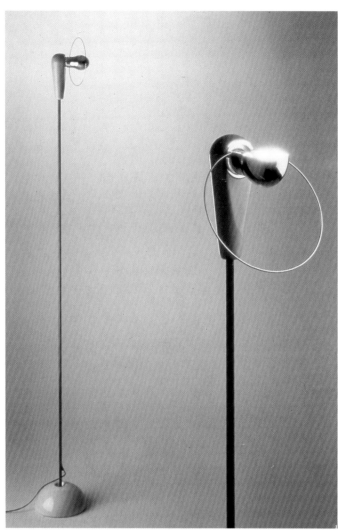

DOCTOR LIFE

Design Philippe Starck 1992
Flos S.p.a.
300 Watt
H 197 cm, B 38 cm
Aluminium, aluminum

Techno-Kitsch: sensationelle Ingenieurs-
verpackung für schlichte Halogenlampe
mit farbiger Filterscheibe

Techno-kitsch: sensational engineers'
shade with coloured filter for simple
halogen bulb

Techno-kitsch: emballage technique sensa-
tionnel pour une simple lampe halogène à
verre filtrant coloré

JAZZ TERRA

Design Andrea Castelli,
Fabio Rezzonico 1989
Segno S.r.l.
50 Watt
H 121 cm, ø 15,3 cm
Metall, Kunststoff
Metal, plastic
Métal, plastique

Fiberglasstab in den Farben Wweiß,
Rot und Blau, Leuchtenkopf beweglich

Fibre-glass rod in red, white and blue;
lamp-head adjustable

Baguette en fibre de verre blanche,
rouge et bleue, tête orientable

COLIBRI

Design Franco Albini,
Franca Helg, Antonio Piva 1984
Sirrah
20 Watt, 12 Volt
H 115 cm, ø 14 cm
Nylon, PVC
Nylon, C. P. V.

TETRAX

Design Mario Bellini 1988
Erco
H max. 264 cm, B 130 cm, ø 126 cm
Aluminium
Aluminum
Aluminium

Verkaufsstrahler auch für das Wohnzimmer:
kommerzielles Warenbeleuchtungssystem,
universell verstellbar

Shop accent light for use in the living-room;
commercial lighting system for goods on
display, universally adjustable

Projecteur pour magasin et salle de séjour:
système commercial d'éclairage des
produits, réglable à tous les niveaux

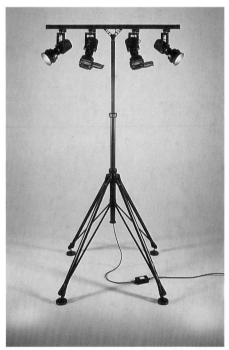

PARENTESI

Design Achille Castiglioni,
Pio Manzù 1970
Flos S.p.a.
150 Watt
H max. 400 cm
Metall, metal, métal

Neofunktionalistischer Strahler, wird
zwischen deckenmontiertem Drahtseil
und Bodengewicht verspannt

Neo-functionalist light on a wire which is
suspended from the ceiling and pulled taut
by a weight on the floor

Projecteur néofonctionnaliste, à tendre
entre un câble monté sur le plafond et un
poids au sol

ELLE

Design Tomasso Cimini 1986
Lumina
300 Watt
H 200 cm / 104 cm
Lackiertes Metall
Painted metal
Métal peint

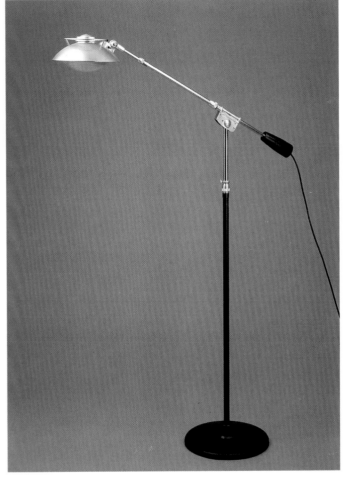

SNODO

Design Hannes Wettstein 1980
Belux
100 Watt
H 130 cm / 60 cm
Metall, metal, métal

ATELIER 709

Design Fernand Solére ca. 1950
Heinze
100 Watt
H 100 - 150 cm
Metall, lackiert, verchromt
Painted metal, chromium-plated
Métal peint, chromé

Kerze, Öllampe und Laterne waren die einfachsten und vielseitigsten Leuchten, weil sie transportabel waren und ohne Reflektoren auf bestimmte Bereiche ausgerichtet werden konnten. Die am weitesten verbreiteten Tischleuchten sind heute die Arbeitslampen für den Schreibtisch. Ihr Urbild, das Modell »Anglepoise«, das dem menschlichen Arm nachempfunden war, stammt von dem Engländer George Carwardine und wurde von Jac Jacobsen als »Luxo L 1« weltweit vermarktet.

Weil Tischleuchten besonders standfest sein müssen, werden sie entweder an der Tischkante festgeschraubt oder mit schweren Füßen versehen. Daher müssen ihre Halterungen oder Arme besonders flexibel sein. Klemmlampen belegen am wenigsten Fläche auf dem Tisch und empfehlen sich besonders für das Büro. Geometrisierende Modelle wie Richard Sappers »Tizio« von 1970 oder Achille Castiglionis »Ipotenusa« von 1974 verdanken ihre Standfestigkeit dem schweren Trafo-Fuß und faszinieren durch die Equilibristik der einzelnen, in der Schwebe verharrenden Gelenke.

Nicht nur zum Arbeiten, sondern auch zum Entspannen eignen sich Tischlampen, wenn ihre Schirme abgewendet werden und sie indirektes, intimes Licht geben. Dekorative Modelle mit Säulen- oder Vasenfuß ähneln oft miniaturisierten Möbelstücken. Wenn sie zudem Textilschirme haben, gelten sie als Inbegriff von Gemütlichkeit.

Candles, oil lamps and lanterns were the most simple and versatile lights because they were portable and could be focussed on certain things without using reflectors. The most common table-lamps are desk-lamps. Their prototype, the Anglepoise, designed by the Englishman George Carwardine and based on the human arm, was marketed world-wide by Jac Jacobsen as Luxo L1.

Because table-lamps have to be particularly stable they are either screwed onto the side of the table or they have a heavy base. Their mounts or arms must therefore be especially flexible. Clamp lights take up the least space on the table-top and are particularly suitable for office use. Geometric models such as Richard Sapper's Tizio (1970) or Achille Castiglione's Ipotenusa (1940) owe their stability to the transformers in their bases, and their fascination to equilibrium of the single and seemingly floating flexible joints.

Table-lamps are not only suitable for working, but also for relaxing; when their shades are turned away they produce an intimate, indirect light. Decorative models with column or vase-shaped bases often look like miniature pieces of furniture. With their cloth lampshades they are considered the epitome of cosiness.

La bougie, la lampe à huile et la lanterne ont été au cours des siècles les luminaires les plus simples et les plus pratiques. Leurs fonctions étaient multiples, on pouvait les transporter facilement et diriger leur lumière sur des points précis. Les lampes de table les plus communes aujourd'hui sont les lampes de bureau. Leur ancêtre, le modèle Anglepoise, créé par l'Anglais George Carwardine qui s'était inspiré du bras humain, a été commercialisé par Jac Jacobsen sous le nom de Luxo L 1. Les lampes de bureau doivent être particulièrement stables, elles sont donc vissées au bord de la table ou équipées de pieds très lourds, par contre leurs fixations ou leurs bras sont très flexibles. Les lampes munies d'un étrier de serrage ne demandent pas trop de place et sont particulièrement indiquées pour le bureau. Les modèles au dessin géométrique comme Tizio, créé par Richard Sappers en 1970 ou Ipotenusa de Achille Castiglioni en 1974 doivent leur stabilité à un pied lourd qui dissimule un transformateur. L'harmonie que dégagent les articulations fixées dans un équilibre aérien est fascinante. Mais ces lampes ne sont pas uniquement destinées au travail: on peut changer la direction des abat-jour, les lampes de table émettent alors une lumière indirecte et intime invitant à la détente. Les modèles décoratifs au pied en forme de colonne ou de vase ressemblent à des meubles en miniature, et s'ils sont aussi garnis d'un abat-jour tronconique en tissu ils deviennent le symbole du confort bourgeois.

CUT

Design Thorsten Neeland 1992
Anta Leuchten GmbH
20 Watt
H 47 cm, B 8 cm,
Aluminium, Schirm: Porzellan
Aluminum, shade porcelain
Aluminium, abat-jour en porcelaine

COSTANZA

Design Paolo Rizzatto 1986
Luceplan
150 Watt
H 76-110 cm, ø 40 cm
Aluminium, Schirm: Siebdruckpolycarbonat
Aluminum, shade: screen-printed polycarbonate
Aluminium, abat-jour: sérigraphie de polycarbonate

Zeitlos und anpassungsfähig: reduzierte
Archetype der klassischen Stehleuchte

Timeless and adaptable: a reduced
archetype of the classic standard lamp

Classique et facilement adaptable:
le lampadaire classique en réduction

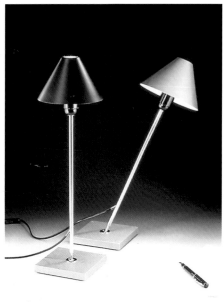

SMALL

Design Daniela Puppa 1992
Fontana Arte
60 Watt, 220 Volt
H 40 cm, B 29 cm, D 10 cm
Kunststoff, Glas, Metall
Plastic, glass, metal
Plastique, verre, métal

GIRA

Design Massana, Tremoleda, Ferrer 1978
Mobles 114
60 Watt
H 53 cm, ø 14 cm
Gußeisen, Aluminium, verchromter Stahl
Cast iron, aluminum, chromium-plated steel
Fonte, aluminium, acier chromé

MISS SISSI

Design Philippe Starck 1991
Flos S.p.a.
40 Watt
H 28,4 cm, ø 14,3 cm
Farbiges Technopolymer
Coloured technopolymer
Technopolymère coloré

Modernes Biedermeier:
Textilschirmimitat aus Ganzplastik

Modern Biedermeier:
imitation textile shade made of shiny plastic

Biedermeier moderne: imitation en plastique
brillant d'un abat-jour en tissu

LAMPARA DE SOBREMESA
Design Antoni de Moragas Gallissà 1957
Santa & Cole
3 x 60 Watt
H 62 cm, ø 44 cm
Holz, Stoffbänder
Wood, cloth strips
Bois, bandes de tissu

BASICA TAMBOR

Design Santiago Roqueta,
Equipo Santa & Cole 1987
Santa & Cole
60 Watt
H 45 cm, ø 40 cm
Holz, Metall, Papier
Wood, metal, paper
Bois, métal, papier

BASICA CÓNICA ALTA

Design Santiago Roqueta,
Equipo Santa & Cole 1987
Santa & Cole
60 Watt
H 65 cm, ø 20 cm
Holz, Metall, Papier
Wood, metal, paper
Bois, métal, papier

BASICA CÓNICA PEQUEÑA

Design Santiago Roqueta,
Equipo Santa & Cole 1987
Santa & Cole
60 Watt
H 45 cm, ø 25 cm
Holz, Metall, Papier
Wood, metal, paper
Bois, métal, papier

LA LUNE SOUS LE CHAPEAU

Design Man Ray 1975
Sirrah
60 Watt
H 62 cm, ø 23 cm
Lackiertes Metall, textilverstärktes Papier
Painted metal, textile-reinforced paper
Métal peint, papier renforcé avec fibres textiles

LANTERNA

Design Alberto Lievore 1992
Gracia Garay
100 Watt
H 57 cm / 38 cm
Holz, Glas
Wood, glass
Bois, verre

MAGNITA

Design Pete Sans 1989
Metalarte
40 Watt
H 30 cm, ø 10 cm
Metall, Gummifuß, Pergament
Metal, rubber base, parchment
Métal, pied en caoutchouc,
parchemin

ARBORICO

Design Roberto L. Lazzeroni 1990
Cidue
60 Watt
H 127 cm, ø 83 cm
MDF, Metall
MDF, metal
MDF, métal

SNOW-LIFT

Design Christian Ghion, Patrik Nadean 1990
Tebong
60 Watt
H max. 72 cm, ø 16 cm
Fuß: Metall, Schirm: Kunststoff kaschiert
Metal base, laminated plastic shade
Pied en métal, abat-jour en plastique contrecollé

WG 24

Design Wilhelm Wagenfeld 1924
Tecnolumen
75 Watt
H 36 cm, ø 18 cm
Metallteile vernickelt, Glas opalüberfangen,
zentraler Schaft aus Klarglas
Nickel-plated metal parts, glass with opales-
cent surface, central shaft of clear glass
Parties de métal nickelées, verre opalisé,
tige centrale en verre clair

Moderner Klassiker mit Bauhaus-Siegel
Modern classic with Bauhaus seal
Classique moderne portant le sigle du Bauhaus

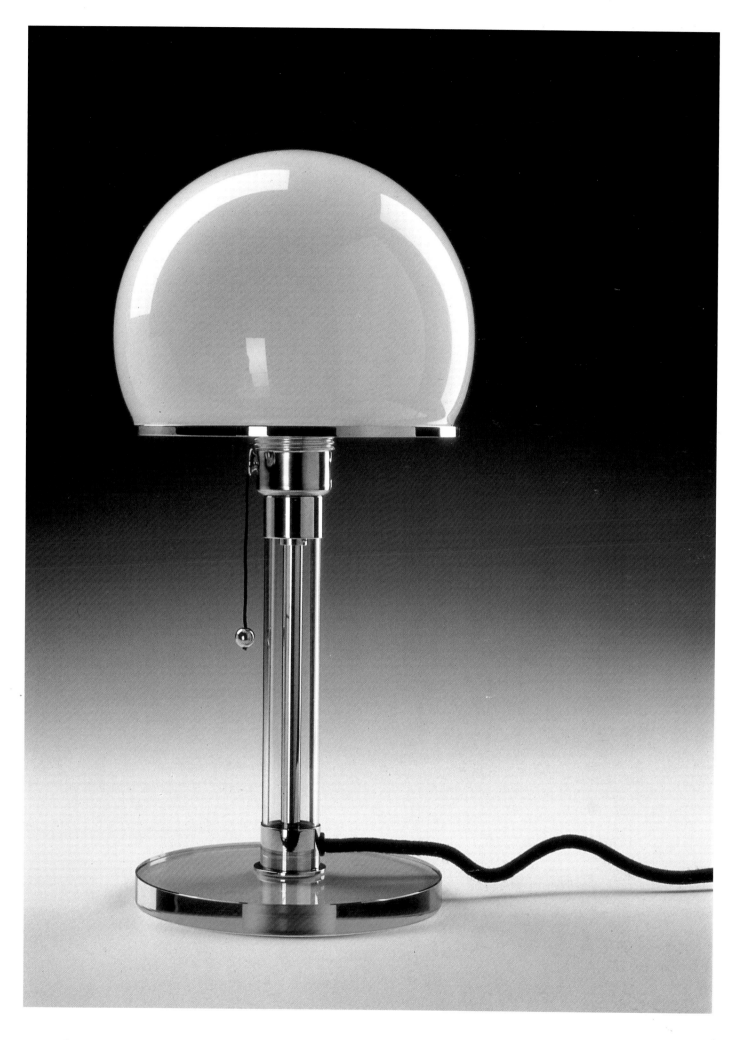

TRAGARA
Design Otto Krüger 1908
ClassiCon GmbH
2 x 40 Watt
H 57 cm, B 82 cm, ø 28 cm
Messing, vernickelt, weißes Opalglas
Nickel-plated brass, white opal glass
Laiton nickelé, verre opalin blanc

Pseudosakrale Wiener Sezessions-Geometrie

Pseudosacred geometry of the
Viennese Secession

Style géométrique pseudo-sacral de
la Sécession viennoise

PH 4-3 TABLE LAMP
Design Poul Henningsen 1966
Louis Poulsen & Co. GmbH
100 Watt
H 55 cm, ø 45 cm
Aluminium
Aluminum

Tischleuchtenvariation der klassischen
skandinavischen Pendelleuchten

Table-lamp variation of the classical
Scandinavian pendant light

Lampe de table inspirée des lampes
à suspension scandinaves

SUNA

Design Jochen O. Becker 1990
Anta Leuchten GmbH
20 Watt
H 70 cm, ø 20 cm
Aluminium, lackiert,
Messing, verchromt, Glas
Painted aluminum,
chromium-plated brass, glass
Aluminium peint, laiton
chromé, verre

FRANCESCINA

Design Umberto Riva 1989
Fontana Arte
60 Watt
H 35 cm, ø 17 cm
Satiniertes Opalglas,
Aluminium oder Messing
Glazed opal glass,
aluminum or brass
Verre opalin satiné,
aluminium ou laiton

BRERA

Design Achille Castiglioni 1992
Flos S.p.a.
100 Watt
H 26 cm, B 14 cm
Glas, Kunststoff, Metall
Glass, plastic, metal
Verre, plastique, métal

111

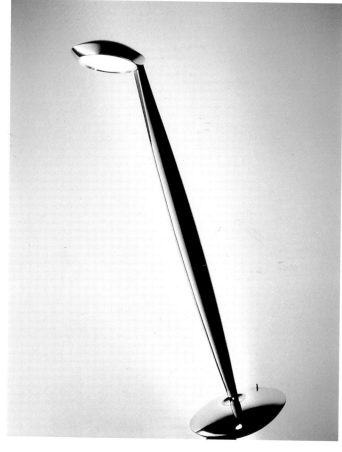

KALLISTO

Design Tobias Grau 1989
Tobias Grau KG GmbH & Co.
100 Watt
H 70 cm, ø 50 cm,
Bronze

TWIST

Design Tobias Grau 1991
Tobias Grau KG GmbH & Co.
35 Watt
H 53 cm
Matt vernickeltes, verchromtes,
schwarzes Metall
Nickel-plated and matte chromium-plated
black metal
Métal noir recouvert
de nickel mat et de chrome

ARÁ

Design Philippe Starck 1988
Flos S.p.a.
35 Watt
H 56,6 cm, ø 17,5 cm
Verchromtes Metall
Chromium-plated metal
Métal chromé

2280 BIS

Design Fontana Arte 1950
Fontana Arte
4 x 40 Watt
H 43 cm, ø 38 cm
Messing, poliert oder lackiert, Mattglas, weiß
Polished or painted brass, white matte glass
Laiton poli ou peint, verre mat blanc

CAPALONGA

Design Tobias Scarpa 1982
Flos S.p.a.
2 x 60 Watt
H 39 cm, B 68 cm
Porzellan, Messing, Metall
Porcelain, brass, metal
Porcelaine, laiton, métal

TACCIA

Design Achille and Piero Giacomo Castiglioni 1962
Flos S.p.a.
1 x 100 Watt
H 54 cm, ø 49,5 cm
Metallsockel, Glasschirm, Kunststoffreflektor
Metal mount, glass shade, plastic reflector
Socle de métal, abat-jour de verre,
réflecteur en matière synthétique

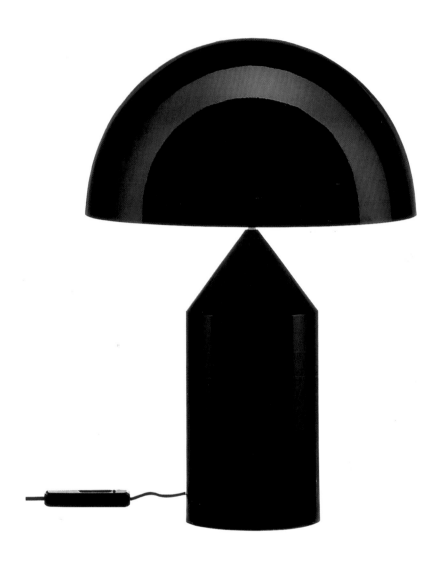

ATOLLO

Design Vico Magistretti 1977
Oluce S.p.a.
2 x 100 Watt
H 70 cm, ø 50 cm
Aluminium, lackiert
Painted aluminum
Aluminium peint

Die Nobilitierung der Büroarbeit :
Repräsentativität für den Schreibtisch

Ennoblement of office-work:
representative lamps for desks

Une lampe représentative qui
ennoblit le travail de bureau

MARIE
Design Jorge Pensi 1990
B. Lux
2 x 20 Watt
H 58 cm, B 40 cm
Aluminium gebürstet, Stahl
Polished aluminum, stainless steel
Aluminium brossé, acier

REGINA
Design Jorge Pensi 1988
B. Lux
2 x 20 Watt
H 58 cm, B 25 cm
Aluminium gebürstet, Stahl
Polished aluminum, stainless steel
Aluminium brossé, acier

BERLINO 90

Design Enzo Catellani 1991
Catellani & Smith
100 Watt, 220 Volt, E 27
H 39 cm, B 18 cm
Messing, Stahl
Brass, steel
Laiton, acier

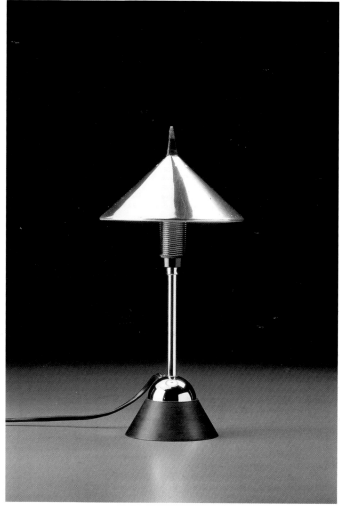

EGON

Design Alberto Lievore 1992
Garcia Garay
75 Watt
H 48 cm
Aluminium, aluminum

MAGNITA

Design Pete Sans 1989
Metalarte S.A.
40 Watt
H 30 cm, ø 15 cm
Metall, Gummifuß
Metal, rubber base
Métal, pied en caoutchouc

COMODINO

Design Yamada Design Studio 1992
ClassiCon GmbH
20 Watt
H 34 cm, ø 10,4 cm
Kunststoff
Plastic
Plastique

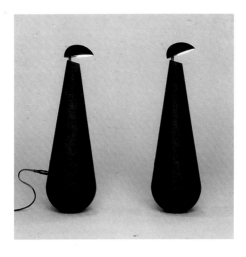

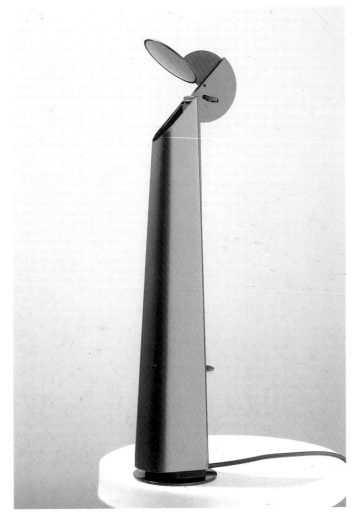

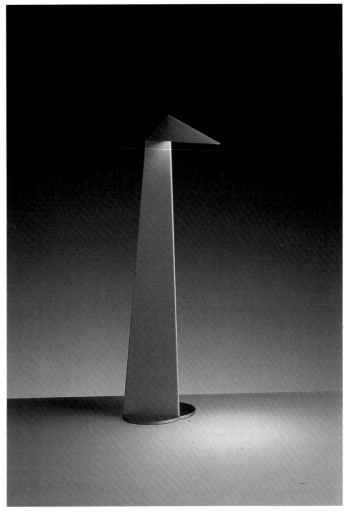

GIBIGIANA

Design Achille Castiglioni 1981
Flos S.p.a.
20 Watt
H max. 52 cm, ø 10 cm
Aluminium, lackiertes Metall
Aluminum, painted metal
Aluminium, métal peint

Reflektorspiegel einstellbar
Reflector mirror, adjustable
Réflecteur-miroir orientable

BIRDIE

Design Jean-Marc da Costa 1990
serien Raumleuchten
50 Watt
H 45 / 54 cm, B 8,5 / 9,5 cm
Stahl, pulverbeschichtet,
schwarz, silber, blau oder türkis
Powder-coated steel,
black, silver, blue or turquoise
Acier recouvert d'une couche de poudre
noire, argentée, bleue ou turquoise

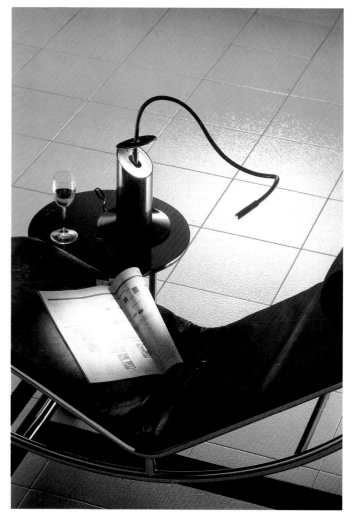

BOLONIA

Design Joseph Lluscá
Metalarte
20 Watt
H 40 cm, ø 14 cm
Metall, mattes, weißes Opalglas
Metal, matte white opal glass
Métal, verre opalin blanc

Miniaturleuchtturm mit zwei entgegen-
gesetzt verstellbaren Lichtquellen

Miniature lighthouse with two light sources
pointed in opposite directions

Phare en miniature: deux sources de lumière
réglables et orientées en sens contraire

ZED

Design Tommaso Cimini 1987
Lumina
20 Watt
H max. 94 cm, ø 18,5 cm
Lackiertes Metall
Painted metal
Métal peint

Gelenkarm mit Akzentlichtpunkt

Jointed arm with accent spotlight

Bras articulé avec spot

AVALON

Design Joseph Lluscà 1992
Blauet
50 Watt
H 25 cm, ø 9,5 cm
Metall, lackiert
Painted metal
Métal peint

TUBO

Design Jo Niemeyer 1984
Belux
50 Watt
L 95 cm
Metall, verchromt
Chromium-plated metal
Métal chromé

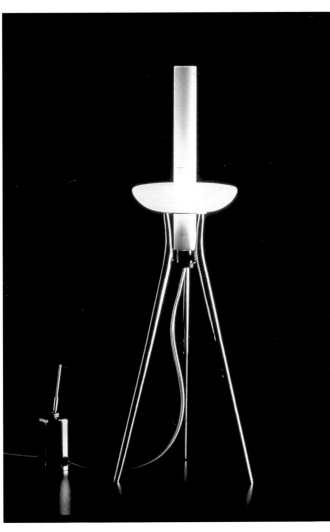

LOREA

Design Jorge Pensi 1990
B.Lux
50 Watt
H 44 cm, ø 15 cm
Metall, sandgestrahltes Glas
Metal, sand-blasted glass
Métal, verre décapé au sable

DAO

Design Lorenza Sussarello,
Guy Brantschen 1990
L´Aquilone
40 Watt
H 75 cm
Metall, Kunststoffgewebe
Metal, plastic tissue
Métal, tissu synthétique

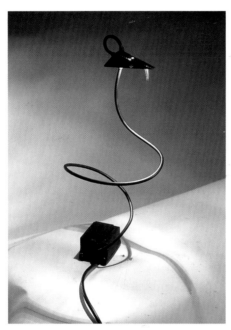

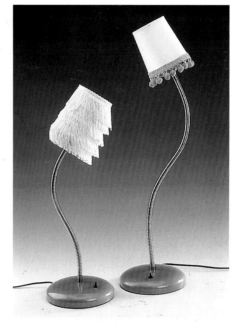

CICLOCINA

Design Enzo Catellani 1991
Catellani & Smith
20 Watt
H 40 cm, L 25 cm
Stahl, Messing
Steel, brass
Acier, laiton

GENOVEVA

Design Georg Alexander Eisenhut 1987
Gio
20 Watt
L 90 cm
Titan, Aluminium, Polyäthylen
Titanium, aluminum, polyethylene
Titane, aluminium, polyéthylène

Achtung Giftzähne!
Beware! Venomous fangs!
Attention, crochets à venin!

SAMBA

Design Lorenza Sussarello,
Guy Brantschen 1990
L´Aquilone
40 Watt
H 65 - 75 cm
Metall, Kunststoffgewebe
Metal, plastic tissue
Métal, tissu synthétique

Neofolkloristische Tütenlampe
auf flexiblem »Schwanenhals«

Neo-folkloristic lamp with conical shades
on flexible »swan's neck«

Lampe tronconique néo-folklorique
sur col de cygne flexible

121

TIZIO 35

Design Richard Sapper 1990
Artemide
35 Watt
H max. 95 cm
Metall und Kunstharz
Metal and synthetic resin
Métal et résine synthétique

Weltweiter Halogen-Bestseller: Design
zwischen Baggerarm und Ölförderpumpe

World-wide best-seller among halogen lamps:
design somewhere between an excavator
arm and an oil-pump

Bestseller mondial des lampes halogènes:
design à mi-chemin entre le bras d'excavatrice
et la pompe à pétrole

TOLOMEO

Design Michele de Lucchi,
Giancarlo Fassina 1987
Artemide
100 Watt, 50 Watt
H max. 123 cm
Aluminium, eloxiert oder schwarz lackiert
Aluminum, electrically oxidized or painted black
Aluminium anodisé ou peint en noir

Weiterentwicklung der
klassischen Gelenkarmleuchte

Further development of the
classic jointed arm light

Perfectionnement de la lampe
à bras articulé classique

LIFTO

Design Benjamin Thut 1984
Belux
50 Watt
H 70 cm
Metall, verchromt
Chromium-plated metal
Métal chromé

DAPHINE

Design Tomasso Cimini 1976
Lumina
20 Watt
H max. 43 cm
Lackiertes Metall
Painted metal
Métal peint

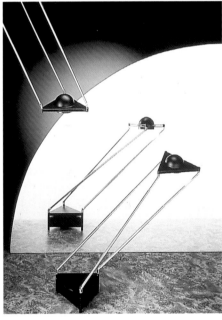

JAZZ

Design F. A. Porsche 1989
Italiana Luce S.r.l.
20 Watt
H max. 56 cm, B max. 60 cm, D 13,5 cm
Technopolymer
Technopolymère

KANDIDO TAVOLO

Design F.A. Porsche 1982
Lucitalia
50 Watt
H max. 86 cm
Aluminium, Kunststoff
Aluminum, plastic
Aluminium, plastique

BERENICE

Design Alberto Meda,
Paolo Rizzatto 1985
Luceplan
35 Watt
H 45 cm
Aluminium-Preßguß, Nylon, Rynite
Die-cast aluminum, nylon, rynite
Aluminium coulé sous pression,
nylon, rynite

672 UNI

Design Elio Martinelli 1992
Martinelli Luce S.p.a.
50 Watt
L 107 cm
Metall, Kunststoff
Metal, plastic
Métal, matière synthétique

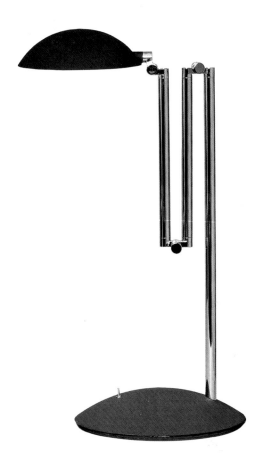

ORBIS
Design Herbert H. Schultes 1991
ClassiCon GmbH
50 Watt
H max. 110 cm
Lackiertes, verchromtes Metall
Painted, chromium-plated metal
Métal peint, chromé

ST 2/400 SR
Design Jean Luis Domecq 1951
Jielde S. A. Lyon
150 W, E 27
L 40 cm, ø 17 cm
Metall, metal, métal

BAP SYSTEM

Design Alberto Meda,
Paolo Rizzatto 1992
Luceplan
11 Watt
H 35 cm / 50 cm, B 30 cm
Polyarilamid, Aluminium, ABS-Kunststoff
Polyarilamid, aluminium, ABS (plastic)
Polyarilamide, aluminium, ABS

Bildschirm-Arbeitsplatzleuchte,
Schwenkarm mit Parallelogrammechanik
(Pantographbewegung)

Lamp for desk with computer, swivel arm
with parallelogram mechanics (pantograph
movement)

Lampe pour poste vidéo, bras orientable,
technique de déplacement du pantographe

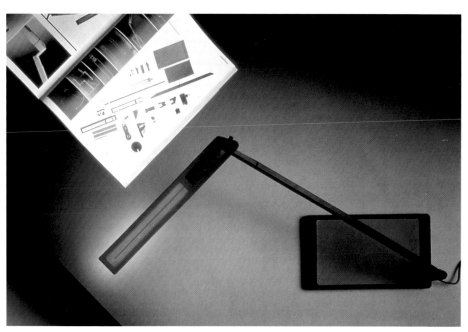

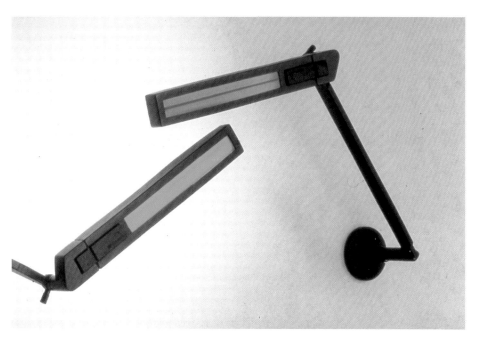

BUMERANG

Design Hannes Wettstein 1981
Belux
11 Watt
H 55 cm , B 31 cm
Metall, lackiert
Painted metal
Métal peint

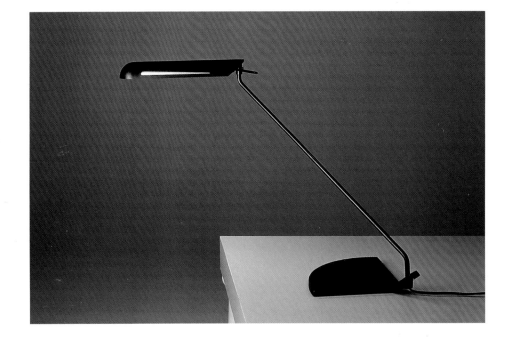

BRAVO

Design Associate Designers 1992
Bravo-U. S.A.
75 Watt
L max. 102 cm
Aluminium, Kunststoff
Aluminum, plastic
Aluminium, matière synthétique

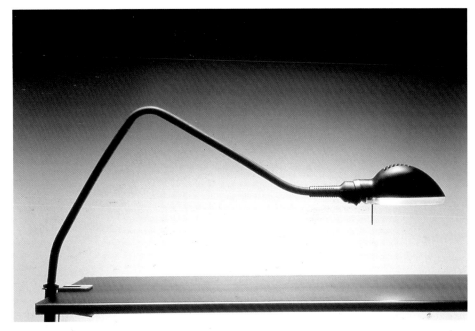

ONIDIA

Design Santiago Calatrava 1992
Artemide
20 Watt
H 45 cm, B 21 cm, D 20 cm
Metall, Thermoplast, lackiert
Metal, painted thermoplast
Métal, matière thermoplastique peinte

Leuchtenkopf verstellbar
Adjustable lamp-head
Tête de lampe réglable

SINI

Design René Kemna 1988
Sirrah
100 Watt
H max. 80 cm
Aluminium, Fiberglas, Sockel aus Zama
Aluminum, fibre-glass, base made of zama
Aluminium, fibre de verre, socle en zama

TANGO

Design Copeland 1989
Flos S.p.a.; koll. Arteluce
50 Watt
L 110 cm, ø 24 cm
Metall, Kunststoff
Metal, plastic
Métal, plastique

IPOTENUSA

Design Achille Castiglioni 1976
Flos S.p.a.
50 Watt
H 55 cm, B 60 cm
Metall, Acrylglas
Metal, acrylic glass
Métal, verre acrylique

Trendsetter der Geometriemode
Trendsetter of the geometric trend
Trendsetter de la vague géométrique

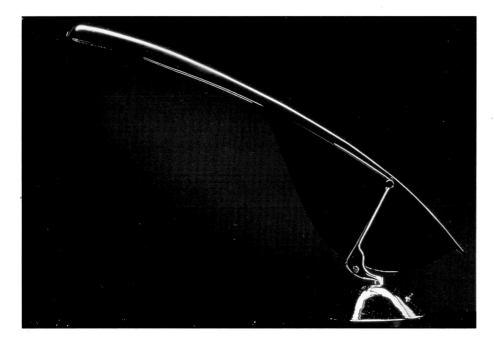

SIMONETTA

Design Massimo Iosha Ghini 1991
B. Lux
50 Watt
B 80 cm
Verchromtes oder vermessingtes
Metall, Buchenholz
Chromium or nickel-plated metal,
beech wood
Métal chromé ou laitonné,
bois de hêtre

129

NIEDERVOLT- UND SYSTEMLEUCHTEN

LOW-VOLTAGE AND SYSTEM LIGHTING

LAMPES BASSE TENSION ET SYSTÈMES D'ÉCLAIRAGE SUR RAILS

Die Lichttechnik hat in den vergangenen hundert Jahren ungezählte Wandlungen erfahren. Der letzte große Umbruch waren die Lichtschienensysteme, die sehr wandlungsfähig sind, unterschiedliche Ausleuchtungen ermöglichen und dabei nur eine Quelle zur Stromeinspeisung benötigen. Dem Systemgedanken ist die Niedervolttechnik am ehesten verwandt. Als erste Anwender gelten die Brüder Piero und Livio Castiglioni, die die »nackte« Lichtquelle als hervorragendes Medium für Weißlicht einsetzen. Doch die anfängliche Primitivtechnik war gefährlich und unbefriedigend und wurde vor allem von den Versicherungsgesellschaften als ein Risikofaktor gefürchtet. Meist wurden die Mono-Leitungen mit 220 Volt geführt und in Reihe geschaltet, so daß beim Ausfall einer Lampe die gesamte Kette unterbrochen war. Kommerziell erfolgreich wurde die Technik erst mit dem von Hannes Wettstein 1984 in Zürich entwickelten Zwei-Schienen-System »Metro« für Belux. Die Schweizer setzten erstmals transformierte Stromstärke ein, die auf dem freigeführten Kabelseil nur noch zwölf Volt betrug. Parallel dazu hatte der Münchner Ingo Maurer sein »YaYaHo«-System entwickelt. Es hebt die Grenze zwischen puristischem Licht und Dekoration auf. Maurer verwendet Klemmen, übergeworfene Gegengewichte und aufgelegte Stäbe, die die Lichtquelle beweglich machen.

Während Niedervoltsysteme sich vor allem für die Wohnung und kleinere Verkaufsräume eignen, sind die Lichtschienensysteme großer Hersteller, etwa Erco oder Staff, vor allem für Büros, Messen und öffentliche Räume bestimmt. Integrierte Deckensysteme haben das Bild heutiger Büroräume maßgeblich geprägt. Die Behandlung der Systemtechnik geht über die vorliegende Darstellung von Leuchten im Interior Design weit hinaus und würde ein eigenes Buch erfordern.

Lighting technology has undergone countless changes throughout the last hundred years. The last great revolution was that of the track light systems, which are highly adaptable. They offer various possibilities of lighting and need only one power point. Low-voltage technology is perhaps most closely related to the idea of system lighting. First to use it were the two brothers Piero and Livio Castiglioni, who found the »naked« bulb was an excellent medium for white light.

The initial primitive technology was dangerous and not satisfactory and was feared as a risk factor by insurance companies. A single cable was usually powered with 220 volts and set up so that the whole chain would be interrupted if a single light-bulb failed. The technique only became commercially successful with the two-track system Metro developed for Belux by Hannes Wettstein in Zürich in 1984. For the first time the Swiss used a transformed current which measured only twelve volts in the free-hanging cables. Parallel to this, Ingo Maurer had developed his YaYaHo system in Munich, which dispelled the distinction between purist light and decoration. Maurer used clamps, hooked on counterweights and balanced rods to make the light source mobile.

While low-voltage systems are suitable for domestic purposes and use in smaller sales areas, light track systems of the big producers such as Erco and Staff are above all intended for use in offices, at exhibitions and in public areas. Integrated ceiling lighting has been a decisive influence on the appearance of today's offices. The subject of system techniques exceeds our presentation of lamps in interior design by far and would require a book in its own right.

Les techniques d'éclairage ont connu de nombreux changements depuis un siècle. La dernière découverte en date est le système d'éclairage sur rails aisément transformable, permettant des utilisations diverses tout en n'ayant besoin que d'une seule source de courant. Son principe de fonctionnement est apparenté à celui des lampes basse tension. Les premiers à avoir tiré parti de cette technique sont les frères Piero et Livio Castiglioni qui considéraient l'ampoule «nue» comme un médium remarquable pour la lumière blanche. Mais la technique était au départ dangereuse, peu satisfaisante et les compagnies d'assurances la jugeaient trop risquée. Les lignes électriques simples étaient le plus souvent placées sous 220 volts et mises en circuit l'une après l'autre, si bien que la chaîne était rompue dès qu'une lampe était hors d'usage. Le succès commercial de cette technique ne survint qu'après la création par Hannes Wettstein en 1984 à Zurich du système à deux rails Metro pour Belux. Les Suisses utilisèrent pour la première fois un ampérage transformé et réduit à 12 volts sur le câble libre. Le munichois Ingo Maurer avait parallèlement élaboré son système YaYaHo qui dilue encore la frontière entre la lumière pure et la décoration. Maurer utilise des pinces, des contrepoids jetés l'un sur l'autre et des baguettes pour donner de la mobilité à la source de lumière.

Alors que les systèmes basse tension conviennent aux appartements et aux petits magasins, les systèmes d'éclairage sur rails des grands fabricants, Erco ou Staff par exemple, sont surtout conçus pour les bureaux, les salons commerciaux et les lieux publics. Les systèmes d'éclairage intégrés dans les plafonds sont partie intégrante des bureaux actuels. Traiter la technique des systèmes d'éclairage demande une étude séparée, car ce livre présente les lampes uniquement dans le cadre de la décoration intérieure.

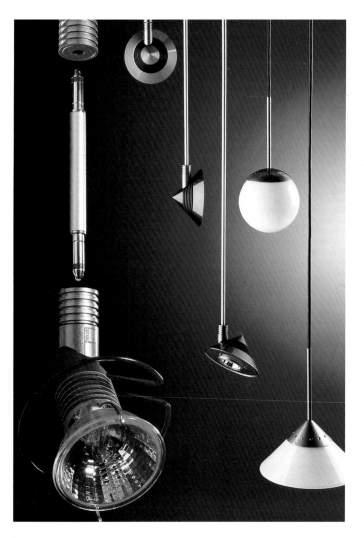

CONTACTO
Design Jürgen Medebach 1990
Belux
50 Watt
Metall, Glas, Kunststoff
Metal, glass, plastic
Métal, verre, plastique

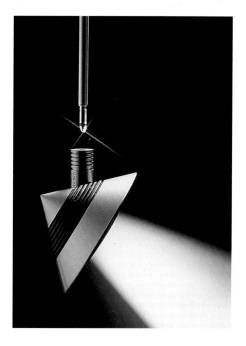

METRO

Design Hannes Wettstein 1982
Belux
50 Watt
Metall, metal, métal

Urahn der im Raum verspannten
Niedervoltsysteme

Early ancestor of low-voltage systems
suspended across the room

Ancêtre des systèmes basse tension
fixés dans l'espace

BAKA-RÚ

Design Ingo Maurer und Team 1986
Ingo Maurer GmbH
50 Watt
Kunststoff, Metall, Keramik
Plastic, metal, ceramic
Plastique, métal, céramique

YAYAHO

Design Ingo Maurer und Team 1984
Ingo Maurer GmbH
50 Watt
Kunststoff, Metall, Keramik, Glas, Porzellan
Plastic, metal, ceramic, glass, porcelain
Plastique, métal, céramique, verre, porcelaine

Verspielte Weiterentwicklungen der verspannten
Niedervoltsysteme zum Technikmakramee

Playful development of suspended low-voltage
systems into a kind of technical macramée

Perfectionnement frivole des systèmes
basse tension en macramé technique

EXPANDED LINE MODULO KIT

Design Perry A. King, Santiago Miranda 1983
Flos S.p.a.; koll. Flight
75 Watt
B 130 cm / 180 cm

Weiterentwickelte Kombination von Lichtschienen-
und Niedervoltsystemen mit vielfältiger Auswahl
von Systembausteinen

Further developed combination of the light track
and low- voltage systems with a wide choice of
system components

Combinaison perfectionnée de systèmes
d'éclairage sur rails et de systèmes basse
tension, éléments modulables

ARCHETTO

Design Matteo Thun 1982
Flos S.p.a.; koll. Flight
50 Watt
H max. 15,5 cm, B 17 cm
Kunststoff
Plastic
Plastique

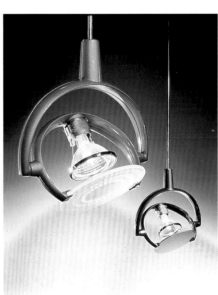

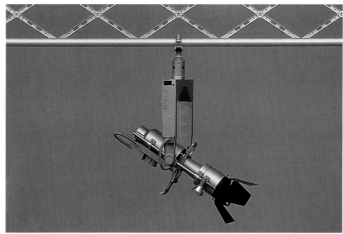

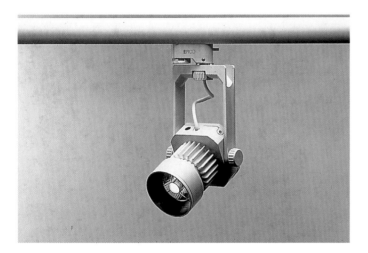

EMANON

Design Roy Fleetwood 1991
Erco
1000 Watt
Aluminium, Metall
Aluminum, metal
Aluminium, métal

ECLIPSE

Design Mario Bellini 1986
Erco
100-500 Watt
Aluminium, aluminum

Ausstellungs- und Warenbeleuchtungs-
systeme, universell verstellbar

Lighting system for exhibition and shop
displays, universally adjustable

Systèmes d'éclairage pour magasin et
exposition, réglables à tous les niveaux

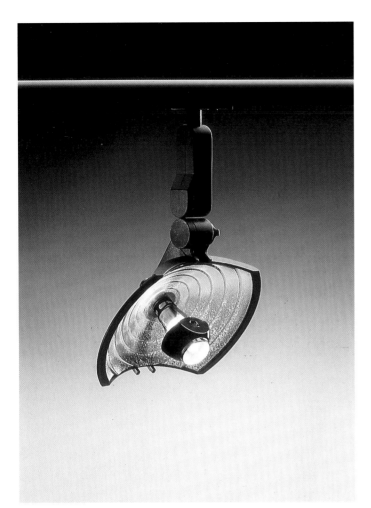

THO

Design Ezio Bellini 1988
Targetti Sankey S.p.a.
50 Watt
H 25 cm, B 16,5 cm, D 100 cm
Ultem, Polycarbonat
Ultem, polycarbonate
Ultème, polycarbonate

Spotleuchte, sowohl einzeln als auch in
Lichtschienensystemen verwendbar

Spotlight, can be used as a single light
or as part of a light track system

Spot à utiliser seul ou sur système
de rails

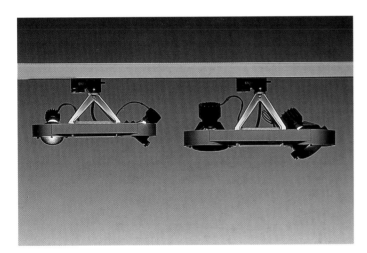

GIMBAL

Design Mario Bellini 1991
Erco
50 Watt
H 13,3 cm, B 30 cm, ø 9,5 cm
H 15,5 cm, B 35,8 cm, ø 12,5 cm
Aluminium, aluminum

BODENLEUCHTEN UND LICHTOBJEKTE

FLOOR LIGHTING AND DESIGN OBJECTS

LAMPES DE SOL ET OBJETS LUMINEUX

Licht diente in der bildenden Kunst immer der illusionistischen Darstellung von Lichtsituationen. Erst in den sechziger Jahren haben Licht und Leuchtkörper eine eigenständige Rolle in der modernen Kunst bekommen, etwa bei den Amerikanern Dan Flavin, Bruce Naumann und Joseph Kosuth oder den Italienern Mario Merz und Pierpaolo Calzolari, die die Signalwirkung von bunten Leuchtstoffröhren für ihre plastischen Arbeiten benutzten. Ein Ableger solcher Lichtkunstwerke und Installationen sind Bodenleuchten und Lichtobjekte für den privaten Bereich. Sie haben eine extreme Ausstrahlung und Kraft im Raum, ohne daß ihre Hauptfunktion im Erhellen liegt. Sie sind halb Möbel, halb Kunstwerk und erzeugen oft eine paradoxe Raumdunkelheit, die den Lichtwirkungen des Kinos nachempfunden ist. Die Grenze zwischen Tisch- und Bodenlampen ist fließend und oft nur von der Größe der Objekte her bestimmbar.

In the fine arts light has always served the illusionistic representation of light situations. Only in the sixties did lights of various sorts adopt an independent role in modern art, for example in the work of the Americans Dan Flavin, Bruce Naumann and Joseph Kosuth, or the Italians Mario Merz and Pierpaolo Calzolari, who made use of the signal effect of coloured fluorescent tubes in their models. A variation of these artistic light creations and installations are floor lamps and design objects for the home. They have a great aura and strength within a room, although their main function is not to shed light. They are half furniture and half works of art, and in a room they often produce a paradoxical darkness based on the lighting effects in cinemas. One cannot always distinguish between table and floor lighting and the distinction is often only made on the basis of size.

Les artistes se sont toujours servis de la lumière pour créer l'illusion. Il a fallu attendre les années 60 pour que la lumière et les corps lumineux jouent un rôle autonome dans l'art moderne, par exemple chez les Américains Dan Flavin, Bruce Naumann et Joseph Kosuth ou les Italiens Mario Merz et Pierpaolo Calzolari qui ont exploité l'effet signalétique des tubes fluorescents multicolores. Les lampes de sol et les objets lumineux d'intérieur sont dérivés de ces œuvres d'art et de ces installations. Leur fonction principale n'est pas d'éclairer, ils n'en ont pas moins un grand rayonnement et une forte présence dans la pièce où ils se trouvent. Mi-meubles, mi-œuvres d'art, ils engendrent souvent une obscurité paradoxale semblable à celle qui règne dans les salles de cinéma. La frontière entre les lampes de table et les lampes de sol est incertaine et c'est souvent le volume de l'objet qui en décide.

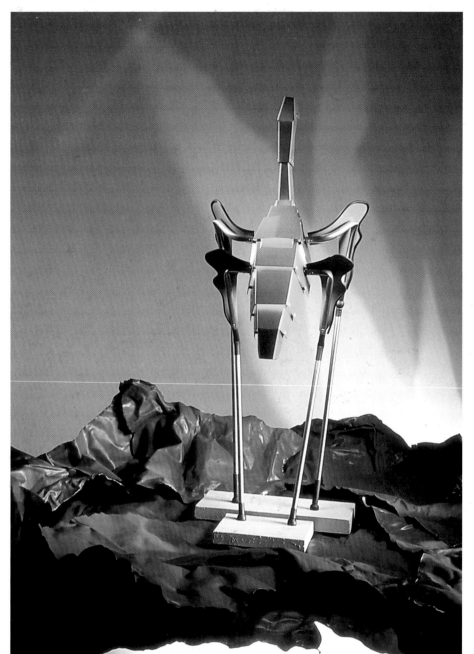

SCARAGOO
Design Stefan Lindfors 1988
Ingo Maurer GmbH
50 Watt
H max. 82 cm, B 33 cm, D 50 cm
Aluminium, aluminum

GISELLE
Design Fumio Shimizu 1991
Driade
50 Watt
H 54 cm, B 14 cm, ø 13 cm
Versilbertes Messing
Silver-plated brass
Laiton argenté

Zoomorphe Fabelwesen, Designungeziefer
Zoomorphous fable creatures, designer beetles
Etre zoomorphe fabuleux, vermine du design

DON QUIXOTE
Design Ingo Maurer 1989
Ingo Maurer GmbH
50 Watt
H max. 45 cm, B 27 cm
Stahl, Aluminium, elastischer Kunststoff
Steel, aluminum, flexible plastic
Acier, aluminium, matière élastique

ONE FROM THE HEART
Design Ingo Maurer und Team 1989
Ingo Maurer GmbH
50 Watt
H 95 cm, B max. 40 cm
Metall, Glasspiegel, Kunststoff
Metal, mirror glass, plastic
Métal, miroir en verre, matière synthétique

CHICAGO TRIBUNE

Design Matteo Thun, Andrea Lera 1985
Bieffeplast
3 x 65 Watt
H 190 cm, B 30 cm, D 30 cm
Lackiertes, perforiertes Metall
Painted, perforated metal
Métal peint perforé

Mikroarchitektur, Wolkenkratzer fürs Interieur

Micro-architecture, a skyscraper for the interior

Microarchitecture, gratte-ciel d'intérieur

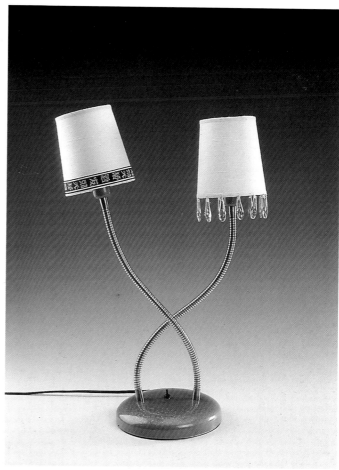

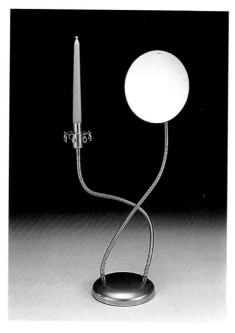

REFLEXE 1

Design Lorenza Sussarello,
Guy Brantschen 1991
L´Aquilone
40 Watt
H 65 cm
Metall, Kunststoffgewebe, Glas
Metal, plastic tissue, glass
Métal, tissu synthétique, verre

Neofolkloristische Lampenbeschwörung
mit Fez und Spiegel

Neo-folkloristic conjuration:
lamp with fez and mirror

Evocation néo-folklorique de lampe
avec fez et miroir

PASO DOBLE

Design Lorenza Sussarello, Guy Brantschen 1990
L´Aquilone
40 Watt
H max. 65 cm
Metall, Kunststoffgewebe
Metal, plastic tissue
Métal, tissu synthétique

REFLEXE II

Design Lorenza Sussarello,
Guy Brantschen 1990
L´Aquilone
H 65 cm
Metall, Glas
Metal, glass
Métal, verre

Neofolkloristischer Kerzenhalter mit
Spiegel auf gemeinsamem Sockel

Neo-folkloristic candle-holder and
mirror on a single base

Chandelier néo-folklorique et
miroir sur socle commun

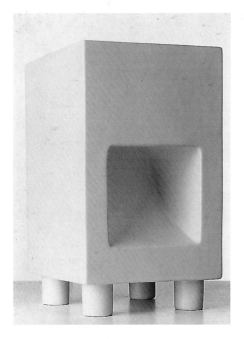

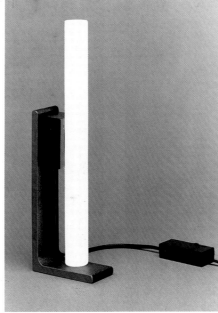

SL 05 LAMPADA

Design Aldo Cibic
Standard STD S.r.l.
40 Watt
H 26 cm, B 16 cm, D 16 cm
Keramik
Ceramic
Céramique

ANGOLO

Design Urs Gramelsbacher 1990
Urs Gramelsbacher
35 Watt
H 31 cm
Eisen, iron, fer

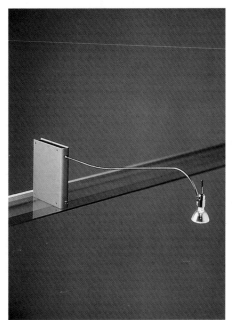

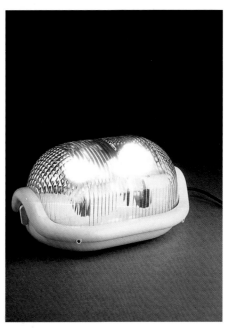

BIB LUZ LIBRO

Design Oscar Tusquets 1985
B. D. Ediciones
50 Watt
B 1,8 cm, L 88 cm
Aluminium, verchromtes Metall
Aluminum, chromium-plated metal
Aluminium, métal chromé

NOCE 1

Design Achille Castiglioni 1972
Flos S.p.a.
2 x 60 Watt,
H 18,5 cm, B 36 cm, D 25 cm,
Lackiertes Aluminium, Preßglas
Painted aluminum, pressed glass
Aluminium peint, verre moulé

ORBITAL TERRA

Design Ferruccio Laviani 1992
Foscarini S.p.a.
5 x 40 Watt
H 170 cm, ø 53 cm
Metall, Glas
Metal, glass
Métal, verre

Fifties-Revival: Lichtskulptur zwischen
Eisdiele und Henry Moore

'Fifties revival: light sculpture somewhere between an ice-cream parlour
and Henry Moore

Nostalgie des années 50: sculpture
lumineuse à mi-chemin entre le café-
glacier et le style Henry Moore

COLLAPSABLES PAPER DRUMS
Design Shiu-Kay Kan 1993
SKK
75 Watt
H 40 cm, ø 30 cm
H 40 cm, ø 40 cm
H 50 cm, ø 50 cm
100% Papier
100% paper
100% papier

AKARI LIGHT SCULPTURES
Design Isamu Noguchi
Ozebi + Co. Ltd.
Mino-gami, Bambus
Mino-gami, bamboo
Mino-gami, bambou

ELASTIC TERRA
Design Karim Azzabi 1990
Oceano Oltreluce
20 Watt
H max. 65 cm, B 22 cm
Kunststoff, Aluminium
Plastic, aluminum
Plastique, aluminum

FALKLAND
Design Bruno Munari 1964
Danese
60 Watt
H 165 cm, ø 40 cm
Elastisches Schlauchgewebe,
weiße Metallringe, Fassung: Aluminium
Flexible hose material,
white metal rings, aluminum mount
Tuyau élastique, anneaux de métal blancs,
cadre en aluminium

WAGAMI ANDON

Design Hiroshi Morishima 1986
Time-space-Art Inc.
40 Watt
H 36 cm, ø 29 cm
H 50 cm, ø 45 cm
H 77 cm, ø 73 cm
Metall, Japanpapier
Metal, Japanese paper
Métal, papier japonais

Fernöstliche Lichtmystik und
Meditationsatmosphäre

Far Eastern light mysticism
and meditative atmosphere

Mysticisme oriental et
ambiance méditative

ZELESTE
Design Angel Jové,
Santiago Roqueta 1969
Santa & Cole
40 Watt
H 40 cm, ø 19 cm
Weißer Alabaster
White alabaster
Albâtre

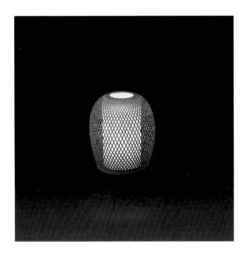

KAZUKI 1
Design Kazuhide Takahama 1976
Sirrah
100 Watt
H 57 cm, ø 33 x 23 cm
Metallbügel, elastische Spezialgewebe
Metal rods, special elastic tissue
Etrier en métal, tissu spécial élastique

FI 4034
DesignYamada Shomei
Yamada Shomei Lighting Co.
40 Watt
H 45 cm, ø 29 cm
Kunststoff, Bambus
Plastic, bamboo
Plastique, bambou

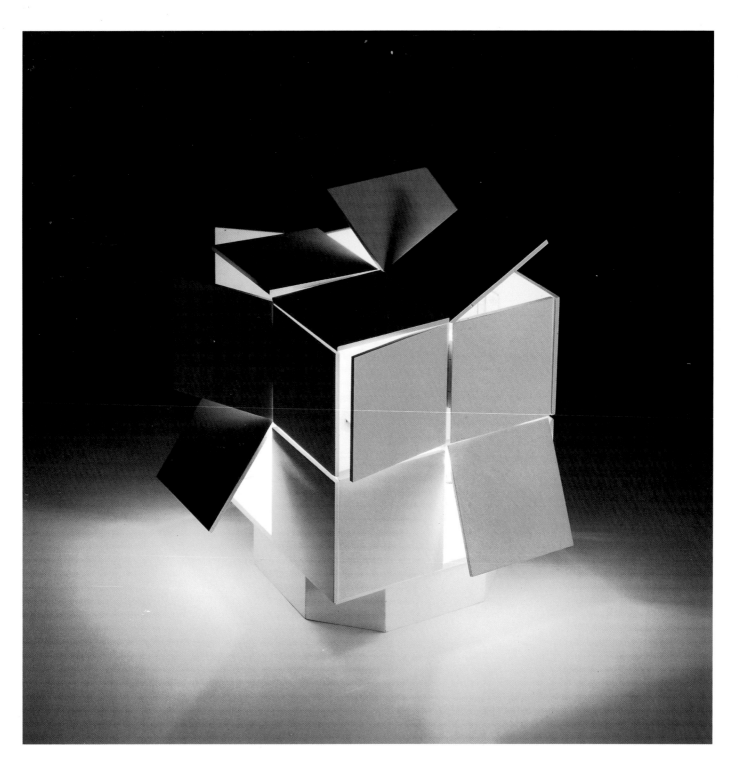

OPEN LIGHT
Design Kaori Shimanaka
Koizumi Sangyo Corp.

Illuminierter Zauberwürfel
Illuminated magic die
Cube magique illuminé

NOTTURNO ITALIANO
Design Dennis Santachiara 1987
Domodinamica S.r.l.
25 Watt
H 17 cm, B 29 cm, D 16 cm
Aluminium
Aluminum

Primitivprojektor für Märchenstunden
Primitive projector for story time
Projecteur primitif pour la veillée

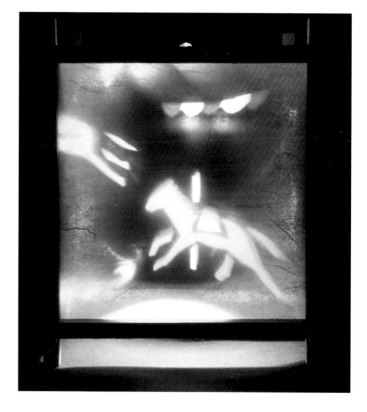

HYDROGEN DREAM
Design Shiro Kuramata 1988
Yamagiwa Corporation
5 Watt, 6 Volt
H 24 cm, B 19 cm, ø 9 cm
Metall, Marmor
Metal, marble
Métal, marbre

Kinetisches Objekt: Das Ein- und Ausschalten
geschieht durch Bewegen des Löffels
Kinetic design object, switched on and off
by moving a spoon.
Objet cinétique: on l'éteint et on l'allume
en bougeant la cuillère

MAGIC LATERN
Design Muji, Shiu Kay Kan 1990
SKK
40 Watt
H 21 cm , B 21 cm, D 21 cm
Papier, Holz
Paper, wood
Papier, bois

Diorama mit drehendem Figurenspiel
Diorama with rotating figures
Diorama avec jeu de figures en rotation

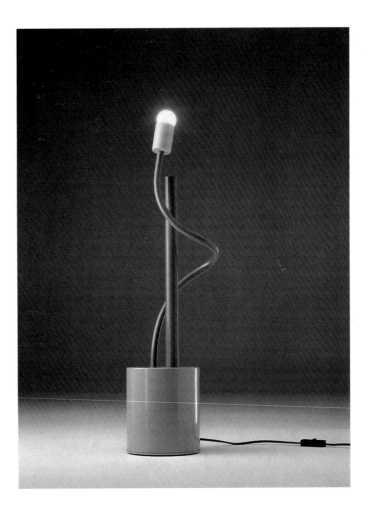

SINER PICA

Design Michele de Lucchi 1979
Belux / Alchemia
40 Watt
H 75 cm, ø 17 cm
Metall, lackiert
Painted metal
Métal peint

Postfunktionalismus:
Topfpflanze als Stehleuchte
Post-functionalism:
Pot-plant as a standard lamp
Post-fonctionnalisme: la plante
en pot devient lampadaire

TOPOLINO

Design Matteo Thun 1989
bieffeplast
16 Watt
H 40 cm, B 34 cm, D 11 cm
Lackiertes Metall, Glasbaustein,
verchromter Griff
Painted Steel, concrete glass,
chromium-plated handle
Acier peint, verre moulé,
poignée chromée

VALIGETTA

Design Matteo Thun 1989
bieffeplast
16 Watt
H 40 cm, B 34 cm, D 11 cm
Lackiertes Metall, Glasbaustein, verchromter Griff
Painted Steel, concrete glass, chromium-plated handle
Acier peint, verre moulé, poignée chromée

Post-Memphis: kommerzialisierte Provokation
Post-Memphis: commercialized provocation
Post-Memphis: provocation commercialisée

SUPER 1981

Design Martine Bendine 1981
Memphis
40 Watt
H 50 cm
Fiberglas, Gummiräder
Fibre-glass, rubber wheels
Fibre de verre, roues de caoutchouc

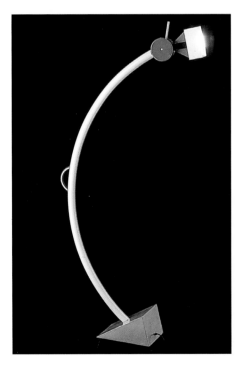

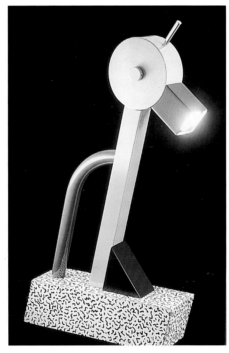

TAHITI

Design Ettore Sottsass 1981
Memphis
50 Watt
H 60 cm
Kunststofflaminat und Metall
Laminated plastic and metal
Laminat synthétique et métal

TREETOPS

Design Ettore Sottsass,
Martine Bedine 1981
Memphis
500 Watt
H 200 cm
Metall, metal, métal

Memphisblüten: Appell an die Sinne
und den Spieltrieb

Blossom of Memphis: an appeal to
the senses and the play instinct

Fleurs de Memphis: appel aux sens
et aux tendances ludiques

LUIGI II

Design Borek Sipek 1988
Driade
50 Watt
L 48 cm, B 15 cm, ø 15 cm
Glas, glass, verre

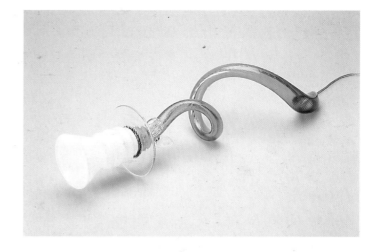

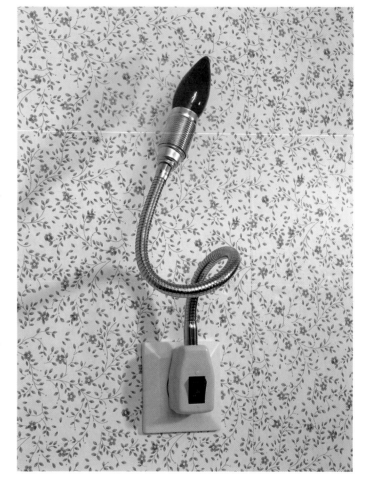

PFLANZLICHT

Design Stiletto Studios 1984
Stiletto Studios
25 Watt
H 10 cm, ø 10 cm
Blumentopf, Leuchtkörper, Erde
Flower-pot, lights, earth
Pot de fleur, lampe, terre

Handsignierte, limitierte Edition von 150 Exemplaren

Hand-signed, limited edition of 150

Edition signée et limitée à 150 exemplaires

GLÜHWÜRMCHEN

Design Stiletto Studios 1990
Stiletto Studios
25 Watt
L 35 cm
Winkelstecker,
verchromter Schwanenhals
Right-angle plug,
chromium-plated swan's neck
Fiche coudée,
col de cygne chromé

T-REX

Design Shiu Kay Kan 1991
SKK
15 Watt
H 35 cm, B 10 cm, D 15 cm
Plastik, plastic, plastique

Fantasy-Echse als Lampenhalter
Fantasy lizard as a lamp-holder
Dinosaure de fantaisie en support de lampe

HERSTELLER

MANUFACTURERS

PRODUCTEURS

Aero Wholesale Ltd.
96 Westbourne Grove
London W2 5RT, England
62

Anglepoise Lighting Ltd. /Tecta
Enfield, Industrial Area GB
Redditch B97 6DR, England
16

Anta Leuchten GmbH
Osterbrooksweg 59
22869 Hamburg-Schnenfeld, Germany
57, 104, 111

Artemide
Via Bergamo 18
20010 Pregnana Milanese, Italy
21, 53, 56, 89, 93, 122, 123, 128

B. Lux
Poligono Eitua S/N
48240 Berrut Bizkaia, Spain
55, 80, 116, 120, 129

B. D. Ediciones
Mallorca 291
08037 Barcelona, Spain
146

Baleri
v. S. Bernadino, 39
24040 Lallio/Bergamo, Italy
95

Belux
Bremgarterstrasse 109
5610 Wohlen, Switzerland
39, 52, 69, 71, 94, 101, 120,
124, 128, 132, 133, 154

Bieffeplast
Via Pelosa 78
35030 Caselle di Selvazzano (Padova), Italy
144, 154

Bilumen
Via Salomone 41
20138 Milano, Italy
48, 87

Blauet S.A.
Aragón, 333
08009 Barcelona, Spain
120

Boréns AB
Barnhemsgatan 15
500 04 Borås, Sweden
43

Bravo-U. S.A.
Poligono Eitua, s/n
48240 Berriz Bizkaia, Spain
128

Castaldi
Via Carlo Goldoni, 18
20090 Trezzano sul Naviglio Milano, Italy
38, 62

Catellani & Smith
Via Antonio Locatelli, 47
24020 Villa di Serio (BG), Italy
50, 73, 96, 117, 121

Cidue Casa Communta S.r.l.
Via san Lorenzo 32
36010 Carré (Vi), Italy
108

ClassiCon GmbH
Perchtinger Straße 8
81379 München 70, Germany
81, 110, 118, 126

Danese
Piazza San Fidele 2
20121 Milano, Italy
149

Design Box
Brückenstr. 2
51379 Leverkusen 3, Germany
74, 75

DLC S. A. »Taller Uno«
Balmes, 11
17465 Camallera, Spain
80

Domodinamica S.r.l.
Alzia Naviglio Pavese 118
20142 Milano, Italy
72, 153

Driade
Via Padana Inferiore, 12
29012 Fossadello di Caorso (Piacenza), Italy
1, 32, 142, 156

Eclipsi
Poligono Industrial, c/A
43800 Valls, Tarragona, Spain
160

Erco
Postfach 2460
58505 Lüdenscheid, Germany
99, 138, 139

Flos S.p.a.
Via Angelo Faini, 2
25073 Bovezzo (Bs), Italy
18, 20, 40, 48, 49, 50, 56, 66, 67,
68, 83, 88, 92, 97, 98, 105, 111,
112, 114, 118, 129, 136, 137, 146

Fontana Arte
Via Alzaia Trieste, 49
20094 Corsico (Milano), Italy
40, 72, 83, 90, 94, 104, 111, 114

Foscarini S.p.a.
Fondamenta Manin 1
30141 Murano, Italy
147

Gio
Lohstraße 28
49007 Osnabrück , Germany
121

Gracia Garay
San Antonio 13, Sta. Coloma de Gramenet
08923 Barcelona, Spain
108, 117

Glaswerke Haller GmbH
Postfach 27
32274 Kirchleugern, Germany
12, 13

Heinze
Röttgen 8
42109 Wuppertal (Elberfeld), Germany
101

Ikea
Bäckgatan
34300 Älmhult, Sweden
16

Ingo Maurer GmbH
Kaiserstr. 47
80801 München 40, Germany
25, 40, 52, 70, 86, 134, 135, 142, 143

Italiana Luce S.r.l.
Via Edison, 118
20019 Settimo Milanese, Italy
124

Jac Jacobsen AS
P.O. Box 60, Manglerud Enebakkvn. 117
0612 Oslo, Norway
16

Jielde S.A.
40, rue Villon
69008 Lyon, France
126

Koizumi Sangyo Corp.
Hase Building 3F, 3-2-8 Bingomachi, chuo-ku
Osaka 541, Japan
152

Kuramata Design Office
1-63-7 Sakura 1- chome, Setagaya-ku
Tokyo 156, Japan
153

Louis Poulsen
Nyhavn 11
1001 Kopenhagen K, Denmark
44, 45, 51, 63, 110

Luceplan
Via E.T. Moneta, 44/46
20161 Milano, Italy
2, 39, 50, 61, 67, 91, 96, 104, 125, 127

Lucitalia
Via Pelizza da Volpedo, 50
20092 Cinisello B., Italy
124

Lumina Italia S.r.l.
20010 Arluno
Italy
50, 87, 100, 119, 124

Luxo Italiana S.p.a.
Via delle More, 1
24030 Presezzo (Bergamo), Italy
84

L´Aquilone
Via Faentina 112
50014 Fiesole Firenze, Italy
87, 121, 145

Martinelli Luce S.p.a.
Via T. Bandetti
55100 Lucca, Italy
71, 91, 95, 125

Memphis
Via Breda 1
20010 Pregnana Milanese, Italy
19, 155

Metalarte S.A.
Apartado / P.O. Box 2439
08080 Barcelona, Spain
53, 54, 78, 84, 108, 117, 119

Mobles 114
Enric Granados 114
08008 Barcelona, Spain
80, 104

Mondo
Viale Brianza 16
22060 Carugo, Italy
8

Nemo S.r.l.
Via Piave 69
22069 Rovellasca (Co), Italy
51, 69, 96

Nieuwenborg/Wegmann
Plantsoen 99 c
2311 KL Leiden, Netherlands
38, 70

Noto / Zeus S.r.l.
Via Vigevano 8
20144 Milano, Italy
71

Oceano Oltreluce
Via Tortona 14
20144 Milano, Italy
149

Odin
Seckenheimer Straße 79
68165 Mannheim 1, Germany
37

Oluce S.p.a.
Via Cavour 52
20098 San Guiliano Milanese (Milano), Italy
115

Ozebi & Co. Ltd.
18, Ogumacho
Gifu-City, Japan
149

Pallucco Italia sas
Via Azzi, 36
31040 Castagnole di Paese (Tv), Italy
82, 90

quattrifolio S.p.a.
Via Kuliscioff, 36
20152 Milano, Italy
69, 92

Radius
Apostelnstraße 24
50667 Köln, Germany
41

Santa & Cole
Santisima Trinidad del Monte, 10
08017 Barcelona, Spain
34, 54, 79, 80, 81, 106, 107, 151

Segno S.r.l.
Piazze dello Sport 9
20015 Parabiago Milano, Italy
87, 99

Sergio Terzani & C.s.n.c.
Via L. Manara, 5/a
50135 Florenz, Italy
72

serien Raumleuchten
Hainhäuser Str.3-7,
63110 Rodgau, Germany
36, 43, 118

Sidecar
Via Bergamo 18
20010 Pregnana, Italy
71, 95

Sirrah
Via Molino Rosso 8
40026 Imola, Italy
41, 48, 60, 66, 86, 99, 107, 129, 151

SKK
34 Lexington St., Soho
London W1R 3HR, England
149, 153, 157

Solzi Luce
Via del Sale, 46
26100 Cremona, Italy
54

Standard STD S.r.l.
Via Carducci 38
20123 Milano, Italy
146

Status S.r.l.
Via Vittorio Veneto, 21/23
20010 Bernate Ticino (Mi), Italy
70, 93

Stiletto Studios
Freienwalder Straße 13a
13359 Berlin, Germany
73, 156

Stilnovo
Via F. Borromini, 12
20020 Lainate / Milano, Italy
35

Targetti Sankey S.p.a.
Via Pratese, 164
50145 Firenze, Italy
139

Tebong
Z.I. Ladeau
35133 Fougeres, France
108

Tecnolumen
Lötzener Straße 2-4
28207 Bremen 1, Germany
41, 42, 53, 68, 109

Tecta
Sohnreystr. 10
37697 Lauenförde, Germany
15

Time-space-Art Inc.
3-17-14 Minami-Azabu, Minato-ku
Tokyo 106, Japan
150

Tobias Grau KG GmbH & Co
Borselstraße 18
22765 Hamburg 50, Germany
35, 58 59, 113

Urs Gramelsbacher
Leonhardsgraben 61
Basel, Switzerland
146

Venini S.p.a.
Fondamenta Vetrai 50
30141 Murano Venezia, Italy
33, 55

Waco
Stapelpein 53
9000 Gent, Belgium
60

Yamada Shomei Lighting Co.
3-16-12, Sotokanda, Chiyoda-ku
Tokyo 101, Japan
46, 47, 66, 151

Yamagiwa Corporation
4-1-1 Sotokanda, Chiyoda-ku
Tokyo 101, Japan
69

SATURNO
Design Juma 1985
Eclipsi
25 Watt
H 40 cm, ø 38 cm
Alabaster, Kunststoff, Metall
Alabaster, plastic, metal
Albâtre, plastique, métal

FOTOGRAFENINDEX
CREDITS
CREDITS PHOTOGRAPHIQUES

Aldo Ballo	71
Bella & Ruggeri	92
Benvenuto Saba	71, 91, 95, 125
Jean Biaugeaud	149
Bictetto/Chimenti	71
Franco Carpa, Livio Ballabio	Delphi, 87, 99
Toon Cousement	60
Luigi Facchinetti	85
Falchi & Salvador	69
Hans Hansen	138
Hiroyuki Hirai	153
Studio Kauffelt, Mannheim	37
Studio Udo Kowalski	45, 51, 63, 110
Rainer Mäntele	36
Marmann, Iserlohn	101
Bernd Mayer, Frankfurt/Main	36, 43, 118
J. Nogai	41, 42, 60, 68
Miro Zaguoli	72, 153
Philips, Eindhoven	26, 27, 28, 29
Pere Queralt	160
Gerrit Schreuers/Nathalie v. Dinther	38, 70
Rudi Schmutz	57, 104, 111
Roberto Sellitto	51, 53, 69, 96
Stalker Studio, Milano	35
Leo Torri	1, 32, 156, 67
Emilio Tremolada	82, 90, 142
Tom Vack, Chicago, Milano	142, 143, 25, 86, 40, 70, 52
Galerie Vallois, Paris	14
Jacqueline Vodoz	148
Wallenhorst/Olböter	121
Michael Wurzbach c/o Fotostudio Kleinhempel, Hamburg	35, 58, 59
Marlboro Design Shop, IDE GmbH	109, 122

ABKÜRZUNGEN / ABBREVIATIONS / ABBREVIATIONS

H	Höhe/height/hauteur
L	Länge/length/longeur
B	Breite/breadth/largeur
D	Tiefe/depth/profondeur
ø	Durchmesser/diameter/diamètre

Der Verlag dankt allen Designern, Architekten und Firmen für ihre freundliche Unterstützung. Insbesondere möchten wir uns bei Frau Ursula Dietz, Milano und Herrn Peter Courtin, Frankfurt bedanken.

The publishers wishes to thank all of the designers, architects and firms for their gracious assistance. We are especially indebted to Ms. Ursula Dietz, Milano and Mr. Peter Courtin, Frankfurt.

Les Editions remercient tous les designers, architectes et entreprises et tout particulièrement Madame Ursula Dietz, Milano et Monsieur Peter Courtin, Frankfurt pour leur soutien amical.